FRIE
and
FOES

FRIENDS *and* FOES

How Congress and the President Really Make Foreign Policy

REBECCA K. C. HERSMAN

BROOKINGS INSTITUTION PRESS
Washington, D.C.

Copyright © 2000
THE BROOKINGS INSTITUTION
1775 Massachusetts Avenue, N.W., Washington, D.C. 20036
www.brookings.edu

Library of Congress Cataloging-in-Publication data

Hersman, Rebecca K. C.
Friends and foes : how Congress and the President really make foreign
policy / Rebecca K.C. Hersman.
p.   cm.
Includes bibliographical references and index.
ISBN 0-8157-3566-9 — ISBN 0-8157-3565-0
1. United States—Foreign relations administration. 2. United States—Foreign
relations—1993—Decision making. 3. United States. Congress—Powers and
duties. 4. Executive power—United States. I. Title.
JZ1480.H47 2000   00-008811
353.1'3'0973—dc21   CIP

9 8 7 6 5 4 3 2 1

The paper used in this publication meets minimum requirements of the
American National Standard for Information Sciences—Permanence of Paper
for Printed Library Materials: ANSI Z39.48-1984.

Typeset in Sabon

Composition by
Betsy Kulamer
Washington, D.C.

Printed by
R. R. Donnelley and Sons
Harrisonburg, Virginia

ℬ THE BROOKINGS INSTITUTION

The Brookings Institution is an independent organization devoted to nonpartisan research, education, and publication in economics, government, foreign policy, and the social sciences generally. Its principal purposes are to aid in the development of sound public policies and to promote public understanding of issues of national importance.

The Institution was founded on December 8, 1927, to merge the activities of the Institute for Government Research, founded in 1916, the Institute of Economics, founded in 1922, and the Robert Brookings Graduate School of Economics and Government, founded in 1924.

The general administration of the Institution is the responsibility of a Board of Trustees charged with safeguarding the independence of the staff and fostering the most favorable conditions for scientific research and publication. The immediate direction of the policies, program, and staff is vested in the president, assisted by an advisory committee of the officers and staff.

In publishing a study, the Institution presents it as a competent treatment of a subject worthy of public consideration. The interpretations or conclusions in such publications are those of the author or authors and do not necessarily reflect the views of the other staff members, officers, or trustees of the Brookings Institution.

Foreword

Conflict between the executive and legislative branches abounds in the making of foreign policy. Everyone involved—executive officials, members of Congress, and "grass-roots diplomats"—must grapple with the changing dynamics of executive-legislative relations.

Rebecca K. C. Hersman, using numerous examples and three case studies from the mid-1990s, illustrates how American foreign policy is really made. She analyzes the transfer of three U.S. ships to the Turkish military; the Brown amendment, which revised proliferation-related sanctions toward Pakistan; and the ratification process for the Chemical Weapons Convention. She offers a practitioner's take, drawn from experience. Her position as special assistant to the under secretary of defense for policy and years on the professional staff of the House Armed Services Committee provided useful vantage points from which to observe the executive-legislative dynamic. She also is fully conversant with the particulars of the cases and examples described here. In addition, she conducted some forty interviews with executive branch officials, congressional staffers, and academic experts.

The author is grateful to the experts and policymakers who shared their insights and experience, almost all of whom did so on the condition that she would not quote them by name. As this book makes clear, much of the foundation for executive-legislative relations is built on informal relationships that are easily undermined by exposure or public criticism. She has tried to provide as rich and informative a description as possible without damaging the trust that permits such dialogue and exchange.

At Brookings the author was a guest scholar in the Foreign Policy Studies program. She is grateful to Richard Haass, program director, for his encouragement, numerous constructive suggestions, and guidance on various revisions. She also thanks James Lindsay, Jeremy Rosner, I. M. Destler, Michael O'Hanlon, Clark Murdock, and others for valuable guidance and suggestions on early drafts of the manuscript.

Theresa Walker edited the manuscript, Helen Winton proofread it, and Shirley Kessel prepared the index. Susan Jackson verified the factual content.

The author completed most of the work on this study while she was an international affairs fellow with the Council on Foreign Relations, and she is especially grateful to the council. Its generosity allowed her to spend a year thinking and writing about the dynamics and processes she had observed during her previous eight years in government.

The views expressed in this volume are those of the author alone and should not be ascribed to the organizations whose assistance is acknowledged above or to the trustees, officers, or other staff members of the Brookings Institution.

MICHAEL H. ARMACOST
President

March 2000
Washington, D.C.

Contents

ONE   *Introduction*

FEW ASPECTS OF U.S. foreign policy are more con-
tentious or controversial than the respective roles and responsibilities of
Congress and the executive in the foreign policy process. Despite the
voluminous efforts of scholars to understand and explain the perpetual
conflict and confusing processes that drive executive-legislative relations
over foreign policy, the debate persists.[1] For foreign policy practitioners,
however, executive-legislative relations are too pervasive and too important to be an academic exercise. The success of their plans and initiatives
often depends on their ability to navigate their way through the executive-legislative minefield.

As history and the Constitution make clear, executive-legislative conflict over foreign policy is inevitable, sometimes even desirable, for it can
provide a degree of checks and balances over ill-conceived or dangerous
policies. Policymakers, however, have good reason to be concerned
about the state of the executive-legislative relationship. While the benefits of these checks and balances are real, the fatigue, frustration, and
mistrust that so often characterize executive-legislative relations can be
devastating to the foreign policy process. Small issues can explode into
big ones over a single misstep, resulting in funding cuts, legal prohibitions, and declining public support. Big issues can succeed or fail
depending on how congressional support is developed and maintained.
When things go wrong, the impact on U.S. foreign policy is real—frayed
relations with critical allies, mixed signals that confuse friend and foe
alike, and diminished U.S. global standing.

1

The challenges of the post–cold war era seem to have exacerbated the anxiety and tension over executive-legislative relations and prompted concerns about U.S. global leadership. The end of the cold war has removed a mantle of gravity and secrecy that insulated U.S. foreign policy and helped to justify and sustain U.S. involvement overseas. Moreover, the lack of a unifying threat has helped to create an impression that the "stakes" involved in foreign policy and defense issues have declined. The power of a globalized economy has realigned the political forces of support for a free trade and internationalist foreign policy and torn down the last vestiges of a wall between foreign and domestic policy. Meanwhile, rapidly expanding access to information is encouraging the spread of "grass-roots diplomacy"—that is, the increasing involvement of players outside the traditional East Coast elite that controlled foreign policy in decades past.[2]

In this complex environment, scholars, pundits, and policymakers look to the public and high-profile battles between Congress and the president as bellwethers of the future of U.S. foreign policy. When Congress supports the president's agenda, as it did with the North American Free Trade Agreement (NAFTA), World Trade Organization (WTO), and North Atlantic Treaty Organization (NATO) expansion, supporters hail the new collaborative spirit and bipartisanship, while opponents accuse Congress of forgoing its deliberative responsibilities and rubber stamping an executive agenda. Similarly, the refusal of Congress to approve fast-track trade authority, the Comprehensive Test Ban Treaty (CTBT), or (for many years) payment of United Nations' arrears is viewed by many as the demise of an internationalist foreign policy and a weakening of executive authority.[3] In the days following the Senate's rejection of the test ban treaty, the president's national security adviser, Samuel Berger, went so far as to accuse Congress of pursuing "a new isolationism" and a "survivalist's foreign policy."[4] Increasingly, policymakers wring their hands, and pundits wag their fingers at a process that seems to grow increasingly complex, politicized, and hostile with each passing legislative season.

The emphasis on institutional conflict and high-profile legislation is understandable. First and foremost, these issues are important. No one can dispute that events such as the approval of the North American Free Trade Agreement or the defeat of the Comprehensive Test Ban Treaty have enormous impact on American foreign policy and credibility. It is also true, however, that the popular media only concentrate on executive-legislative relations in times of crisis or conflict. As a result, many observers are simply not aware of the full depth and breadth of executive-legislative relations. Furthermore, political scientists, in their search for more quantitative and statistical means of evaluating executive-legislative relations, have often focused on those congressional actions that constitute institutional views, namely, recorded votes and official legislative actions. These are times when institutional action and interbranch conflict are most evident.

Legislation can shape the landscape of executive-legislative relations in dramatic ways, especially when it appears to signify a major shift in the foreign policy powers. For many policymakers, legislation such as the Lend-Lease Act of 1941, the 1964 Gulf of Tonkin Resolution, or the 1975 Arms Export Control Act all marked critical junctures in U.S. foreign policy and represent significant shifts in the balance of power between Congress and the executive. This is the legislation of which legend is made. Legislative and executive-legislative crises affect not only the substance of U.S. foreign policy but also the views and values of the individuals involved. Policymakers recount their involvement in the battles over the Turkish embargo in 1974, aid to the Nicaraguan rebels during the mid-1980s, or important free trade legislation of the 1990s like war stories. The perceptions and impressions of these events die hard, if ever.

Big votes and sweeping legislation tend to grab the headlines and frame the debate about the state of executive-legislative relations, but they only tell part of the story. A focus on these high-profile events tends to produce a formal, institutionalized portrait of Congress that bears little resemblance to the practical, day-to-day reality of most policymakers. In reality, the executive-legislative dynamic is not nearly so dramatic or so easily explained. In between these highs and lows, the majority of foreign policy churns on below the noise and largely out of the public eye. Trying to evaluate the state of executive-legislative relations according to these headline-grabbing events is like trying to measure an ocean by counting waves. Dramatic clashes over high-profile issues— "waves"—are important, but they do not tell all, or even most, of the story. It is in the "ocean"—the day-to-day interactions over unexceptional issues—where most foreign policy is shaped, debated, and made.

Why should we care about these more obscure issues and interactions? After all, some might argue that these are mundane, bureaucratic interactions over secondary issues—not the fundamental clashes that shape and redefine the balance of power between the branches or significantly alter the course of U.S. foreign policy. The ocean, however, does matter. First, many foreign policy issues never receive public attention and media scrutiny or trigger broader institutional clashes, yet their impact on important elements of U.S. foreign policy or key bilateral relationships is considerable. Working these issues is the time-consuming, energy-intensive business of foreign policy professionals in both branches.

Second, the way that conflicts are handled down in the policy "trenches" has an enormous influence on whether they evolve into broader, high-profile institutional conflicts. As in all dynamic relationships, conflict between the executive and legislative branches tends to escalate as a result of early misunderstandings and miscalculations. While some high-profile conflicts may be inevitable, many are not preordained and can be minimized or even prevented if they are handled more effectively in earlier stages.

Finally, even large, high-profile conflicts are built on a base of routine and informal interactions. These issues ebb and flow, popping onto the national radar screen as the stakes mount and actions intensify, only to fall back again as the moment of crisis passes. Often, the fate of these high-profile battles can be determined as much by how the issue is handled in the trenches as by what happens to it once it hits the political stratosphere.

The Informal Universe, Issues, and Individuals

For the most part, policymakers struggle within porous, fragmented institutions where policy is driven more by like-minded individuals than by disciplined organizations, conflict is as much intrainstitutional as it is interinstitutional, and issue loyalties often outweigh partisan ties or institutional allegiances. In this environment, relations between the branches are characterized as much by collaboration and negotiation as by confrontation and conflict, a reality understood by a few insiders but often misunderstood by a majority of the foreign policy community. This book identifies several keys to understanding these institutional dynamics and their impact on U.S. foreign policy.

The Informal Universe

It is impossible to understand how much of U.S. foreign policy is shaped and debated without acknowledging the power of the informal universe. Much of the interaction between Congress and the executive occurs outside of the formal legislative process and official channels of communication. In fact, so rich is this informal interaction that often policy is influenced and changed before more formal processes are even initiated. Votes, hearings, and legislation—the traditional business of Congress—only tell part of the story. Use of the media, informal procedures, commitments, and relationships—the essential elements of the informal universe—are crucial to the foreign policy process.

By using the informal universe, issue leaders can dramatically expand the manner and extent of their policy influence by shaping the issues or leveraging executive branch behavior. Members of Congress (especially in the Senate) use informal and procedural powers to advance or obstruct the legislative process. The importance of the informal universe, however, is not limited to the legislative branch. The executive branch relies heavily on unofficial processes to vet ideas, ascertain congressional hostility, or request assistance. Sometimes, even formal legislative action is little more than a ratification of the informal negotiations and agreements that have preceded it. In other cases, Congress and the president have established informal patterns and routines, which, though not legislatively binding, carry considerable force of practice and precedent.

Both branches of government also use both public and private communications in hopes of shaping policy decisions, even when their direct impact on policy may be limited. Letters, opinion pieces, talk show appearances, floor statements, press releases, and personal phone calls are part of the daily dialogue between the branches. The informal universe has always been a critical element of executive-legislative relations, but given the pressures of near instantaneous communications, an ever-shortening news cycle, and an increasingly cumbersome legislative process, its role can only increase.

Institutional Weakness and Individualized Power

Another essential element of the executive-legislative dynamic over most foreign policy is the idiosyncratic and personalized nature of the process. The historic institutional battles between Congress and the executive over the control of U.S. foreign policy belie the power that individuals are able to grasp and exercise. Today, institutional fragmentation and ideological polarization sharply limit strong institutional leadership over foreign policy, while the expansion of informal and procedural powers enhances the power of individuals.

Such individualism on the part of members of Congress is not new, but several ongoing trends have steadily exacerbated it. First, during the past several decades, institutional reforms have redistributed power and weakened the committees that used to dominate congressional involvement in foreign affairs. The days when the views of a few powerful committee chairs could dictate an institutional response are long gone. Second, partisan cleavages and ideological polarization seriously complicate efforts to build a majority in favor of a traditional internationalist foreign policy agenda and often render "party discipline" almost irrelevant to the foreign policy process, especially on those issues that remain largely below the surface and out of the public eye. As a result, members of Congress and their staffs face few constraints from institutional structures or partisan dictates as they pursue many of their individual foreign policy interests. Finally, the informal universe inherently favors individual power. As a result, growing procedural and informal powers, combined with a crowded legislative calendar and an unwieldy legislative process, have greatly enhanced the individualized nature of executive-legislative relations over foreign policy.

Issue Leaders

Individualized power explains much about "how" Congress influences foreign policy, but it fails to explain "who" is inclined to do so. In the absence of strong institutional roles or partisan loyalties, foreign policy leadership is determined more frequently by issue leaders than by office holders. Any member of Congress with the personal drive and interest to champion an issue can become an issue leader. Leaders can include key office holders, such as committee or subcommittee chairs, but such positions, while often enhancing the individual's leverage over the executive, are not required if the member is adept at manipulating the informal universe.

The importance of issue leaders is not an entirely new phenomenon. Individuals in Congress have long used informal and individual powers to champion or oppose issues. Several factors, however, seem to be increasing the prevalence and importance of leaders. First, the end of the cold war and dissolution of the Soviet Union have eliminated an analytical and budgetary framework that provided structure, urgency, and priority to U.S. foreign policy. As the "stakes" connected with congressional involvement in foreign policy have declined, so too have the disincentives associated with policy entrepreneurship and single-issue advocacy.

In addition, the American public remains profoundly disinterested in foreign policy.[5] Given the lack of political salience associated with foreign policy, declining interest in foreign affairs is more evident in Congress and, some would say, even in the presidency. As a result, fewer members are focusing on foreign affairs, but those few who do are playing a disproportionate role. Finally, in the 1990s U.S. foreign policy has grown more complex, and the distinctions between foreign and domestic policy have steadily evaporated, bringing a greater number of issues and players into the foreign policy mix. Increasingly, foreign policy issue leaders may champion their foreign policy concerns and interests from their positions on the banking, finance, judiciary, or environment and natural resource committees, which have far more cachet with constituents and voters.

Cross-Institutional Linkages

At the formal, institutional level, conflict dominates executive-legislative relations over foreign policy. For most foreign policy issues, however, a different and more complex relationship emerges. Congress and the executive are neither as hostile nor as separate as they appear. The executive and legislative branches are intertwined not merely by the powers they share but also by the nature of the institutions and the individuals who inhabit them.

Although at one level these institutions are highly adversarial, the individuals that compose them are closely linked into informal relationships and networks. Huge quantities of information move informally—back-channel—between these institutions every day. When operating constructively, these relationships and networks provide the avenue for preventing or solving problems through informal consultation and collaboration. At times, however, these same networks allow controversy and debate from within the executive branch to "spill over" to Congress, as disaffected parties seek another audience for their views or concerns. In almost all cases, congressional issue leaders rely on sympathetic elements of the executive bureaucracy for advice, information, and even advocacy of their position or concern within the interagency process.

Issue Clusters

Institutional linkages, however, cannot be viewed in isolation. These informal relationships and networks are not solely the domain of the federal government. Rather Congress and the executive branch coexist with interest groups, nongovernmental organizations (NGOs), and even state and local governments as "issue clusters" to advocate for certain policies and interests. It is not uncommon for clusters of collaborators from Congress, the executive, and nongovernmental entities to team up against similar issue clusters with opposing views. These different entities rely on one another for information, advice, and early warning about opposing interests. In many foreign policy debates the conflict lies less between Congress and the president than between two different issue clusters with competing visions for U.S. foreign policy. This set of complex and crosscutting relationships defines "reality" for most policymakers.

Studying the Ocean

Studying these executive-legislative relationships at the sometimes mundane, day-to-day level poses several challenges. Informal power does not leave much of a paper trail or lend itself to statistical analysis. Moreover, much of the informal collaboration between Congress and the executive is off the record. In fact, the relationships that allow such collaboration are often unacknowledged or off-line. Public recognition of these relationships could result in lost contacts or sources, accusations of institutional disloyalty, or even punitive action by that person's home institution. Therefore, while institutional conflict between Congress and the executive over foreign policy tends to be more public and documentable, more collaborative interactions tend to be informal and secretive. As a result, descriptions of informal and procedural dynamics are unavoidably dependent on anecdotal information and descriptive cases.

This book relies extensively on three case studies and numerous other examples to illustrate the institutional dynamics that drive much of today's foreign policy process. The first one describes a little-known but high-impact controversy involving the transfer of three naval frigates to Turkey. This case is a typical example of how individual power and informal agreements can drive policy and generate controversy (largely outside of the legislative process), while never really becoming a public or high-profile institutional dispute. The second case—the battle to obtain congressional approval to loosen proliferation-related sanctions on Pakistan—shows how both Congress and the executive can operate in the ocean even when official actions and formal legislation are required. While this controversy contained several waves, including a fairly high-profile vote and considerable media attention during its later phases, this issue was handled and debated largely within a community of foreign policy professionals whose issue loyalties far outweighed partisan or institutional allegiances.

The third case describes the highly acrimonious battle to secure Senate ratification of the Chemical Weapons Convention. A classic wave, the ratification of the Chemical Weapons Convention ultimately became a high-profile, politicized contest between the president and a deeply divided Congress. The sixty-seven votes required for ratification combined with the potent procedural powers of the Senate posed a daunting challenge to ratification of the treaty. As the election season approached, high-profile attention to the treaty increased the stakes, and political intensity associated with the treaty rose dramatically. Despite its high-profile, institutional characteristics, however, informal power, intimate cross-institutional relationships, and powerful issue clusters still played a vital role, especially during those times that the issue fell out of the headlines and back into the hands of the issue leaders driving the process.

These examples typify the important and frustrating issues that absorb the attention of both senior and midlevel policymakers on a routine basis—the bread-and-butter issues of executive-legislative relations on foreign policy. Each in its own way illustrates the depth and variety of congressional power and executive-legislative interactions over foreign policy. While all three cases deal primarily with security issues, they all differ significantly from one another in visibility, intensity, legislative requirements, and manner of congressional influence. Despite these differences, the five keys to understanding how Congress and the executive interact over foreign policy—the informal universe, individualized power, issue leaders, institutional linkages, and issue clusters—are evident throughout.

TWO   *Individual Power*
       and Issue Leaders

In 1960 Richard Neustadt challenged the formalistic approach to studying presidential power, claiming "the constitutional convention of 1787 is supposed to have created a government of 'separated powers.' It did nothing of the sort. Rather, it created a government of separated institutions *sharing* powers."[1] Therefore, according to Neustadt, the president's power derives less from his formal legal authority and more from his "power to persuade" Congress and other entities that claim a role in government to follow his direction.[2] Neustadt argued that in a system of shared powers, presidential leadership and authority depend less on a constitutional mandate and more on the president's abilities as a leader and a negotiator. Neustadt attributed these informal and persuasive powers to the president, but they are no less applicable to members of Congress and other executive branch officials who seek to advance their foreign policy agenda in a fractured, individualized, and informal environment.

In part because of these informal and persuasive powers, individualized power has come to rival institutional or structural power when it comes to congressional influence over U.S. foreign policy. At one level, the individual nature of Congress's involvement in foreign policy is widely acknowledged. Derisive, almost cliched, references to the "535 secretaries of state" that inhabit Capitol Hill have been evident since the 1970s. One long-time staffer and member of the Clinton administration offers a more useful analogy: "There are 535 sole proprietors in Congress, all accountable to their constituents and no longer accountable to or protected by larger institutional or political structures."[3]

This "sole proprietorship" can be explained by several ongoing trends. First, during the past several decades, institutional reforms actively sought to democratize both the House and Senate by empowering the rank and file and weakening the seniority-based committee system. These processes, combined with more recent changes in the policy environment that have made membership on the foreign affairs committees politically unattractive, have taken a heavy toll on the committees that traditionally exercise oversight over foreign policy matters. This individualized power is enhanced by the array of informal powers and procedural tactics that members of Congress and their staffs may use to drive (or more often obstruct) the legislative process, limit executive action, or frame the public debate. At the same time, deep divisions within the major parties over foreign policy and a growing ideological polarization in Congress prevent the national parties from providing strong, consistent leadership on these issues. While less severe than in the legislative branch, institutional fragmentation is also increasingly evident within the executive branch. As this chapter explains, neither united government nor renewed bipartisanship is likely to rescue U.S. foreign policy from this rising tide of individualized power any time soon.

In this fragmented, informal, and ideologically polarized environment, issue loyalties often overshadow partisan or institutional allegiances and "issue leaders" rather than institutional office holders drive the policy process. Issue leaders, those members or congressional staffers willing to use all the formal, procedural, and informal powers at their disposal to champion or oppose specific issues, are essential to understanding how Congress engages in the foreign policy process.

Individualized Power

Between the late 1930s and the mid-1960s, congressional power largely rested in the hands of "an oligarchy of senior leaders, sometimes called 'the barons' or 'the old bulls.'"[4] These members, primarily committee chairmen, operated in a closed and secretive system and could "generally be expected to speak on behalf of Congress."[5] Institutional reforms, particularly in the House, during the past three decades have weakened the seniority system, fragmented the committee structure, and dispersed power to members of the rank and file.[6] By opening pro-

ceedings to public scrutiny, expanding the authority of the party cau-
cuses, and reducing the concentration of power within the committee
chairs, both Houses of Congress significantly reduced the concentration
of power previously vested in the committee structure. The process was
less formal in the Senate but nonetheless resulted in what Senate scholar
Barbara Sinclair calls a transition from "decentralization [power vested
in committee chairmen] to individualism."[7] These trends have reinforced preexisting inclinations and traditions in the Senate, which favor
individual power.

More recent efforts at reforms have done little to arrest this underly-
ing trend. In 1995, following the Republican takeover of Congress,
Speaker of the House Newt Gingrich undertook several reforms
designed to provide greater centralization of power in the House by
strengthening the House leadership. This expansion, however, came
largely at the expense of an already weakened committee structure. It is
true that the Republican leadership gave committee chairmen more control over staff and subcommittee chairs and assignments, but as congressional scholar Barbara Sinclair explains, "These new rules that tended to
strengthen committee chairs . . . were, however, more than counterbal-
anced by new rules tending to weaken them."[8] These new rules included
limiting all chairmanships to three two-year terms, banning proxy voting, and further limiting the chairman's ability to close a committee
meeting.[9] One long-time staffer and current administration official
explained the matter more starkly, saying, "Gingrich's reorganization
decimated the committees."[10]

By further centralizing power in the leadership, these reforms also
encouraged "decisions that are more politically-driven than policy-
driven, making foreign policy more vulnerable to domestic political
linkages."[11] Former Representative Lee Hamilton has decried the
expansion of such linkages saying, "The policy of creating linkage
between difficult and unrelated issues has been raised to an art form in
recent years."[12] Political linkages, such as one between UN funding and
the abortion issue, are extremely difficult, however, without the strong
support of the leadership. As a result, these political distortions of the
policy process are more evident on those few high-profile, highly contentious issues that rise to the attention and involvement of the leadership. These reforms have been less significant for the lower-profile,
bread-and-butter issues of foreign policy, which rarely garner such high-
level attention.

The 1998 end-of-year appropriations process is a perfect example of this bifurcated process. Congress proved unable to pass many of the thirteen annual appropriations bills individually in a form the president would sign. With elections looming just over the horizon, the congressional leadership once again elected to negotiate an "omnibus" appropriations bill that would combine the remaining appropriations requirements into one end-of-year bill—a technique that has become increasingly common. This enormous $500 billion "catch-all" appropriations bill resulted from backroom negotiations among a very small number of senior White House aides, representatives of the House and Senate leadership, and a few other key lawmakers. That small group of negotiators handled all the top-priority issues, including a few foreign policy priorities such as the Chemical Weapons Convention implementing legislation, the $18 billion in additional funding for the International Monetary Fund (IMF), and the supplemental funding for Bosnia peacekeeping operations.[13]

For those issues that made the list of high-priority concerns to be included in the negotiations, this process was the epitome of highly centralized power. But aside from these high-profile issues, what happened to all the other foreign policy concerns on the fiscal year 1999 agenda? With the traditional committee-based appropriations process not working, these matters had to be handled more informally, individually, and invisibly than ever. In general, this sort of highly centralized approach ensures that power is highly concentrated for a few high-profile issues but even more fragmented and individualized for most others.[14]

Although power in the executive branch is not nearly as fragmented and individualized as it is in Congress, political scientists have long known that the executive branch is rife with bureaucratic politics that divide it into competing departments, agencies, and even individuals.[15] As will be explained in greater detail in chapter 3, these subcomponents play a major role in how the executive branch develops and communicates foreign policy. At one level, the executive branch is traditionally expected to present unified, formal positions (namely, the president's or the administration's policy) regardless of internal disagreements and divisions. Only rarely, however, does the executive branch truly speak with one voice. In theory, everyone in the executive branch is required to support the president's budget upon submission to Congress. And in public they usually do. Private, informal discussions, however, often produce a very different result. In addition, formal administration positions (often referred to as "Statements of Administration Policy") tend to gloss over disagreement and debate within the executive and are most relevant to the "formal process" of determining the president's position on legislation that will come to a vote. That said, Congress is subject to no similar pretext of institutional uniformity. Moreover, all of the senior-most officials in the executive branch serve at the discretion of the president, which does give the president considerable power to demand a degree of institutional loyalty, at least in public.

Institutional fragmentation is evident within the executive branch as well. As U.S. foreign policy has grown increasingly complex and distinctions between foreign and domestic policy begin to evaporate, foreign relations are no longer solely, or even principally, the domain of the Department of State. Today an increasing number of executive branch departments and agencies have international responsibilities and overseas programs. The Department of Treasury, with its lead responsibilities toward the International Monetary Fund, was the dominant player throughout the Asian financial crisis. The National Aeronautics and Space Administration has ongoing space cooperation programs with Russia. The Department of Justice and the Federal Bureau of Investigation lead terrorism investigations, such as the investigation of the Khobar Towers bombing in Saudi Arabia, thereby becoming a major actor in U.S. relations with a key strategic ally. The FBI also has a growing number of overseas program and training activities, particularly in eastern Europe and the former Soviet Union. The Defense Department supports humanitarian assistance, disaster relief, threat reduction, and numerous programs with foreign militaries. With this many players in the foreign policy process it is hard for the executive to speak to foreign governments, let alone the U.S. Congress, with one voice.

Decline of the Foreign Affairs Committees

Congressional reforms in the 1970s deliberately sought to reduce the power of the full committee chairmen by transferring power to the subcommittees. Following these reforms, subcommittees could "write their own rules; employ their own staffs; and meet, hold hearings, and act on legislation."[16] The 1994 reforms restored some of these powers to the full committee chairs, but these changes were designed to enhance the role of the committee chairs "relative to other committee members, not relative to the leadership."[17] As mentioned earlier, the combined effect was the substantial weakening of the committee system. This trend has been acute among the foreign affairs committees—the House International Relations Committee (HIRC) and the Senate Foreign Relations Committee (SFRC). These committees no longer play the dominant role they once did.

In part, the weakness of the traditional foreign affairs committees can be attributed to the quality of their leadership. Long-time SFRC Chairman Claiborne Pell's passive leadership opened the door for other senators, most notably Senator Sam Nunn (D-Ga.), then chairman of the Senate Armed Services Committee, to step into the leadership vacuum. Current SFRC Chairman Jesse Helms (R-N.C.) has reasserted some control over the committee, particularly through his aggressive use of the nominations process, but his many contrarian foreign policy views prevent him from becoming the Senate's foreign policy "spokesman." Similar problems have limited the HIRC. In 1995 Speaker of the House Newt Gingrich played a large role in key committee assignments, hand-picking a number of strong members to lead key committees to ensure that they would support the goals of the Republican leadership. The House International Relations Committee was not one of the priority committees, and the committee has languished under the leadership of Benjamin Gilman (R-N.Y.).

In addition, the inability of the House and Senate foreign affairs committees to pass any comprehensive authorizing legislation for the nation's foreign assistance budget since 1985 has sharply reduced their relevance, particularly compared with the foreign operations subcommittees, which now both authorize and appropriate most foreign assistance funding. The reasons for this breakdown in the authorization process are numerous. First, foreign aid is politically unpopular. Getting a majority in the House and Senate to pass an aid authorization bill without an unacceptable level of concessions or costly linkages to unrelated issues has proved extremely difficult. Once legislators get out of the authorization habit, it can be extremely difficult to get back into it. Why take two painful votes on foreign aid (one to authorize and another to appropriate), when one will do?

Furthermore, the operating expenses for the State Department and other foreign affairs agencies are authorized separately in the State Department authorization bill. Traditionally this bill has been considered "must pass" legislation because of a statutory requirement to authorize appropriations for the department's operating expenses. By separating this bill from the foreign assistance legislation, foreign assistance has often lacked an "engine" to pull it through the legislative process.

Today, even the State Department authorization bill is a less reliable legislative vehicle than in the past. Before 1995, State Department authorization bills were passed on a fairly consistent basis. From 1996 to 1998, however, Congress was unable to pass a State Department authorization bill in a form that was acceptable to the president. For those three years the requirement for authorization was waived in the Commerce, Justice, and State appropriations bill. For fiscal year 1999, a State Department authorization bill was folded into the 1999 omnibus appropriations bill.[18] As one frustrated former staffer exclaimed, "For years you always had a State Authorization bill, even if the foreign assistance act did not make it. Now even that bill isn't a sure thing."[19] Without a reliable vehicle on which to concentrate these issues, lawmakers tend to address their foreign affairs concerns in a more isolated fashion, either as independent legislation or as amendments to a wide variety of other legislation. In this kind of process, there are few checks on limiting or negative legislation (limits, reports, sanctions, prohibitions, and so on) dealing with specific issues, and few incentives for "positive" legislation or administration requests.

Moreover, as responsibilities for foreign affairs proliferate throughout the executive branch, each government agency brings its oversight committee further into the fray. As a result, the Commerce, Finance, Judiciary, Banking, and Ways and Means committees are playing a greater role in international affairs than ever before. Says a long-time House International Relations Committee staffer, "Members can work on foreign policy from almost any committee; they don't need to be here to work their issues."[20]

This process stands in sharp contrast to the defense authorization process. The Department of Defense has one comprehensive authorization bill, which generally passes every year. Issues tend to be concentrated and negotiated on that single bill, and both branches of government have a strong interest in fashioning an acceptable version. The committee aggressively asserts its jurisdiction and resists (with a relative degree of success) authorizations on the appropriations bill.[21] More important, as one long-time observer explains, "Defense has a built-in constituency—veterans across this country and the vast military-industrial complex—that comes to the fore whenever that bill is threatened.

The pressure to pass that bill is huge, so the threat of a presidential veto or a stalled-out process carries a lot of weight."[22]

Without the crisis atmosphere of the cold war, foreign policy often finds itself on the political "back burner." Except for a few "hot-button" issues, foreign policy lacks broad-based political salience. In fact, most Americans continue to be profoundly disinterested in and ill-informed about international affairs.[23] With a track record of limited legislative accomplishments and responsibility for issues with little hometown appeal, the foreign affairs committees do not offer appealing assignments for many lawmakers. In the House, where membership on the foreign policy committees is viewed almost as a political liability, recruiting and keeping dynamic new members has become especially difficult. As one House staffer explains, "Members serve on the International Relations Committee almost as an avocation. They have a keen personal interest in foreign affairs and serve at the risk of their constituents."[24] Former Minority Staff Director Michael Van Dusen agrees, adding, "Not many members are interested in foreign affairs. It is no longer prestigious. Our committee members can't take much home politically."[25]

In the Senate, many senior members have avoided the committee, leaving many committee positions in the hands of relatively new members. In 1999 first-term senators chaired all seven of the SFRC's subcommittees. Some observers attribute this development to the disinterest of more senior members, arguing that "with the Cold War over, veteran senators prefer domestic committees."[26] Between the "unusual latitude" given to these senators by committee Chairman Jesse Helms's and Senate Majority Leader Trent Lott's (R-Miss.) relative disinterest in foreign affairs, this diverse set of junior senators has unusual influence. One such senator, Chuck Hagel (R-Neb.) along with Senator Pat Roberts (R-Kans.), led the Senate effort to replenish the IMF reserves. Senator Hagel actively sought out his seat on the Senate Foreign Relations Committee and assumed the chairmanship of the Subcommittee on International Economic Policy.[27]

Senator Roberts has lambasted Congress, the president, and the public for the current state of affairs saying, "Not since the 1930's, when Congress passed the neutrality acts just as the world was going up in flames, not since the Smoot-Hawley tariff helped create the Great Depression, has Congress been so insular and isolationist in its view of the world. Not since the 19th century has an administration been so lacking in foreign policy focus, purpose and constructive agenda. Not in our lifetime has the American public been so uninterested and uninformed about world events."[28] Clearly, these senators are trying to redirect the Republican Party back to its internationalist roots. It is too soon to know if these efforts are merely exceptions to the new political reality or if they represent the emergence of a new internationalist leadership in the Senate.

Procedures, Prerogatives, and Informal Power

Congress, as an institution, usually speaks its will by voting. While votes can constitute an important measure of congressional sentiment and institutional power, observers must use caution in the meanings they attach to congressional votes. The number of truly contested votes that result in a clear institutional position on a particular foreign policy issue are few and far between. Votes are often highly orchestrated "games" and not all votes are created equal. Sometimes, voting outcomes do not necessarily constitute a genuine institutional view. Once it is clear what the outcome of a vote will be, other members may cast their vote differently in response to political or constituent pressures, making a vote look much narrower or more lopsided than it actually was. Moreover, particularly in the House, members often cast their vote confident that the language will be modified or eliminated during the House-Senate conference, or in the case of some stand-alone legislation, that the Senate may never act on the provision.

From 1991 to 1996, the House repeatedly voted overwhelmingly in support of fairly draconian burdensharing legislation sponsored by Chris Shays (R-Conn.) and Barney Frank (D-Mass.) during debate on the defense authorization bill. The language was usually softened in conference following extensive, high-level lobbying by the executive branch. Members found it difficult to vote against legislation that was popular with constituents and supported by influential organizations such as the American Taxpayers Union, even if they disagreed with the foreign policy implications of such legislation. Once Representatives Frank and Shays had the votes necessary for passage, many other members did not want to take the political heat for opposing the legislation when they could not affect the outcome. Every year the conferees sharply curtailed the legislation, but the conference report encountered little difficulty during final passage.

Similarly, opponents of a provision sometimes will follow a deliberate strategy of including the provision in a bill (often as part of an "en bloc" amendment of supposedly uncontroversial provisions) to avoid an unfavorable vote on the floor. They will then work closely with staff and conferees on a bill to get the language removed or modified once the House-Senate conference has begun. Many legislative strategists believe that by avoiding an unfavorable recorded vote, the members will have greater flexibility to modify or even remove the provision during the House-Senate conference. More important, many of the most important contests cannot be analyzed on the basis of "contested votes," since the vote was never taken. For example, if the supporters of a given bill think that the vote is going against them, they will often withdraw the legislation rather than suffer defeat. Such was the case with the fast-track legislation in the fall of 1997 and with the first scheduled vote on the Chemical Weapons Convention in September 1996. Forcing the proponents of a measure to accept a negative vote without an opportunity to withdraw, as happened with the Comprehensive Test Ban Treaty, is still the exception rather than the rule.[29]

Observers must not only observe caution when weighing the significance of recorded votes, they must also give sufficient weight to the many ways that members of Congress and their staffs influence policy that cannot be easily measured or recorded. Public hearings provide another traditional and effective forum to confront the executive over major foreign policy issues. Such hearings have a long and storied history. Senator J. William Fulbright's televised hearings on Vietnam in 1966 greatly contributed to the groundswell of public opposition to the war and helped to trigger the political transformation that occurred a few years later. In 1975 the hearings and reports issued by the Church committee (named after its chairman, Senator Frank Church, D-Idaho) and the Pike committee (named after its chairman, Representative Otis Pike, D-N.Y.) fundamentally altered the role of the intelligence agencies in U.S. national security and established permanent congressional oversight over U.S. intelligence activities.[30] In 1990 the House Armed Services Committee, chaired by Les Aspin (D-Wisc.), held a series of hearings on the Persian Gulf crisis that greatly helped to garner congressional support for President George Bush's decision to use military force to evict Saddam Hussein's troops from Kuwait.

Legislation and hearings are by no means the only ways that Congress influences foreign policy. Members of Congress exert influence over foreign policy through many formal and informal mechanisms, including informal inquiries, investigations, floor statements, and various procedural customs and techniques.[31] Often combined with the threat of future legislation, these tools can afford individual members significant influence over policy by leveraging the executive branch without resorting to the formal legislative process. Members also participate in "framing"—that is, engaging in "efforts to shape public and elite opinion" with the intention of influencing policy outcomes.[32] Any member of Congress can make use of his or her office as a "bully-pulpit" to persuade the executive branch, fellow members, and even the public to support his view. Floor statements, television appearances, public speeches, newspaper op-eds, and all other forms of dialogue with the public give members numerous opportunities to make their case and test their ideas every day. These activities are potent weapons in a member's informal arsenal.

Far less understood and appreciated by much of the policy community and the public are the ways that lawmakers and their staffs use informal procedures, agreements, and procedural techniques to influence the executive branch. Interestingly, this type of informal power is especially potent on the foreign affairs committees. Despite (perhaps even because of) the difficulties these committees face in passing legislation, the State Department can ill-afford to provoke the ire of these members and their staffs, especially on many day-to-day issues. Hostile and punitive legislation or embarrassing hearings and reports remain a significant threat. In addition, the foreign affairs staffers have cultivated close relationships with their counterparts on the foreign operations appropriations subcommittee. As a result, members and staff on the authorizing committees can issue credible threats on funding cuts, fences (limits on funding pending some action, usually a report, by the executive) and other restrictions. Authorizers and appropriators, despite their contentious relationships, can often find common ground when it comes to opposing the executive branch.

To manage these informal dynamics, Congress and the executive rely on traditions and habits that have developed over the years to preserve smooth working relationships. For example, in the area of conventional arms transfers, the State Department honors a largely unwritten yet extensive notification system designed to keep members and their staffs fully apprised of expected transfers. The entire U.S. foreign aid program is rife with such requirements, but security assistance activities stand out. U.S. security assistance, for example, is subject to as many as thirty-six different types of reports and notifications.[33] Many of the notification requirements are not legislated but rather have developed informally over time.

One such arrangement is the twenty-day "prenotification" of prospective arms sales that would trigger the notification required by section 36(b) of the Arms Export Control Act. These include sales of "major defense equipment for $14 million or more, defense articles or services of $50 million or more, or design and construction services for $200 million or more."[34] This requirement dates back to a 1976 agreement between the Defense Department and Congress and has remained in effect ever since. The Department of State adheres to the system religiously, and a simple call from a staffer warning about congressional concern or asking for additional information is usually enough to bring the proposed transfer to a temporary halt.[35] Such requests by members or their staffs to delay action on a given issue are commonly referred to as "holds." The fact that officials in both branches refer to these requests for delay as holds simply underscores how seriously requests are taken. A hold by a member, especially if it is conveyed in writing, is almost never ignored even though it is not legally binding. "Preconsultation" is a more recent innovation. This process involves addressing all congressional concerns and securing a tentative approval from the minority and majority staffs of the House International Relations Committee and the Senate Foreign Relations Committee before forwarding 36(b) arms transfer notifications.[36]

In the Senate, a simple majority is no longer really meaningful on most legislation since it requires unanimous consent or a super majority of sixty votes (to invoke cloture) to allow a floor debate. As a result, the overwhelming majority of Senate business is conducted according to a unanimous consent. Unanimous consent agreements, which require the acquiescence of every senator, can detail the terms (time for debate, number and types of amendments, and so on) under which legislation will be considered. Once agreed to, these agreements also require unanimous consent to be changed.[37] When unanimous consent is not possible, only a vote by sixty or more senators to invoke cloture can curtail an individual senator's right to unlimited debate and delay. The cloture process is difficult and time-consuming, and even after a successful cloture vote, debate may continue for another thirty hours, a near eternity in a compressed and overcrowded legislative calendar.[38]

Senators exercise their rights to extended debate by using various powerful, procedural tools, particularly filibusters and legislative holds, which are designed to enhance individual power and preserve minority rights. These devices significantly increase the ability of congressional issue leaders to drive policy or at least to obstruct it. Legislative holds and filibusters have evolved over time such that one senator can force the legislative process to a near standstill. Individual senators filibuster a bill when they invoke their right to unlimited debate and thereby prevent a measure from coming to a vote. A senator does not have to hold the floor in the manner Jimmy Stewart made famous in *Mr. Smith Goes to Washington* to make use of the filibuster. Merely expressing the intention to do so to the Senate majority leader is sufficient. To break a filibuster, the legislation's proponents must garner a "supermajority" of sixty votes to invoke "cloture" and thereby impose limits on debate.[39] Once reserved for extreme circumstances, the use of filibusters has expanded dramatically since the early 1970s. According to one recent study, while "only 23 manifest filibusters are recorded for the entire nineteenth century, the number totaled 191 between 1970 and 1994."[40] The explosion in the use of filibusters for obstructionist purposes prompted former senator Charles Mathias to proclaim that "the filibuster has become an epidemic."[41]

A senator need not "filibuster," however, to exercise individual power in the Senate. Short of that, a senator may use a legislative hold to delay legislation from coming to a vote. Legislative holds differ from the holds on executive action described earlier. Because of the centrality of unanimous consent agreements to the daily operations of the Senate, a senator may place a hold on legislation simply by registering an objection with the Senate leadership. As a matter of tradition, holds are anonymous and therefore are difficult to measure.[42] The use of holds increased dramatically in the 1970s and since that time have been used increasingly for the purpose of obstructing legislation rather than simply alerting the leadership to legislation of interest.[43] Holds can delay all forms of legislative business, but they have been used to particularly obstructive effect in the nomination process. For example, repeated holds by Senator Chuck Grassley (R-Iowa), Senator Mitch McConnell (R-Ky.) and Senator George Voinovich (R-Ohio) on the nomination of Richard Holbrooke to become the U.S. ambassador to the United Nations delayed the confirmation process by more than fourteen months.[44]

Partisan Politics and Foreign Policy

Unfortunately, those who seek to replace institutional fragmentation on foreign policy with party discipline are likely to be disappointed. "Party loyalty" has always been a tenuous force on most foreign policy issues. Franklin D. Roosevelt battled extensively with fellow Democrats over foreign policy, hitting a low water mark with congressional passage of the Neutrality Act in 1937. In 1947 President Harry S. Truman sought and received approval of some of the most important foreign policy legislation of the twentieth century, such as the NATO Treaty and emergency aid for Greece and Turkey, from a newly elected Republican Congress. During the Carter administration, Democrats were surprised and disappointed that unified government did not bring about greater unity in foreign policy.

In 1978 Indiana Representative Lee Hamilton and his aide Michael Van Dusen described this process saying, "When President Carter was elected in 1976, with apparently clear-cut Democratic majorities in both houses, some observers predicted that the problems of friction between Congress and the executive would be reduced. . . . In hindsight, this was never in the cards."[45] Hamilton and Van Dusen go on to say, "We would venture that it is almost a law of contemporary American politics that a Republican President with a majority is under great pressure from the extreme Right, while a Democratic President is under similar pressure from his liberal constituency. If a President finds—as both Gerald Ford and Jimmy Carter have recently found—that foreign problems rarely yield to extreme approaches, he needs the opposing party to neutralize his own zealots."[46]

During the first two years of the Clinton administration, Democrats enjoyed the first unified government in twelve years, and expectations that unified government would dampen executive-legislative conflict over foreign policy again ran high. Once again, such expectations were dashed. Between 1992 and 1994 relations between the Clinton administration and the Democratic Congress were highly acrimonious, especially on foreign and defense policy. As one executive branch official describes the period, "The Democrats thought that we would cut off IMET [International Military Education and Training], put human rights at the top of the agenda, and do other things that key congressional Democrats had been pushing for years. But the bureaucracy took over, and the administration backtracked on many of its election season promises. The rift between what they [Congress] wanted from us, and what we [the administration] expected from them was enormous. We expected them to fall into line, and they expected the administration to deliver on all their old pet projects."[47]

Big foreign policy successes such as Russian aid, the World Trade Organization (WTO), and NAFTA depended extensively on Republican support. Meanwhile, congressional Democrats often failed to support the administration's policies toward Bosnia and Somalia or the United Nations. Of course, members of the president's party would try to avoid votes that might publicly expose rifts or "embarrass" the president. Such cooperation on legislative tactics, however, often obscured the angry exchanges and bitter negotiations that were occurring behind the scenes. Democratic members wanted to avoid a political spectacle but were perfectly willing to challenge "their" president when they could do so through informal and procedural devices that kept the challenge out of the public eye.

Much the way that united government has failed to deliver an expected degree of agreement between the branches on foreign policy, divided government has been less destructive than at first it may appear. As mentioned earlier, many of the greatest foreign policy achievements have been the result of divided government.[48] Moreover, even periods of extreme hostility and conflict have had unpredictable results. For example, during the first year of the new Republican Congress in 1995, executive-legislative relations descended into open warfare on many fronts, especially on domestic issues. The foreign policy battles, however, were remarkably contained.

The Republican ten-point "Contract with America" that laid out the initial agenda for the new Republican majority contained one point on foreign policy, a fairly vague requirement to restrict U.S. involvement in peacekeeping and to deploy an antiballistic missile system.[49] In February 1995 the House debated HR 7 (National Security Restoration Act), the much-touted foreign policy analogue to the "Contract with America," which included provisions to curtail U.S. funding of UN peacekeeping and limit the president's ability to place U.S. troops under foreign commanders. Most of the bill's language, however, was rhetorical, and even the command and control provision included a presidential waiver. More onerous restrictions, such as the one that would have barred assignment of U.S. forces to UN operations without prior congressional approval, were eliminated during floor debate. In fact the HR 7 debate dealt Republicans their first major defeat on the contract when the

House rejected, 218 to 212, a provision that would have directed the United States to develop and deploy a space-based antimissile defense system. The bill passed the House on February 16, 1995, but never really went anywhere in the Senate.[50]

For all its anguish and intense conflict on many high-profile issues, the difference between the Democrat-controlled Congress and the Republican-controlled Congress in terms of support for the president's foreign policy agenda was less dramatic than the rhetoric would suggest. The fiscal year 1996 legislative cycle—the year of the "shutdowns"— was profoundly contentious at the institutional levels. Nevertheless, even in this hostile environment, the administration pushed through a number of foreign policy priorities. These included a substantial foreign assistance package for Jordan and the Warsaw Initiative, which provided funds to help member countries participate in the Partnership for Peace, a 1994 Clinton administration initiative designed to expand "political and military cooperation beween NATO and the former Soviety bloc."[51] In addition, the Republican leadership often had difficulty keeping its junior members in line. Many of the new Republican freshmen bucked their leadership and the committee chairmen on foreign policy and defense issues by delaying or rejecting key bills and conference reports, such as the fiscal year 1996 defense appropriations.[52]

Clearly, today's hostile and deeply partisan political climate affects relations between the branches. As one congressional scholar explains, "The business of political parties is to oppose each other, to defeat each other, to discredit each other, all of which is normal and healthy. But when different parties control different elements of government, this healthful competition is transmuted into conflict between institutions of government themselves."[53] Yet in several ways, divided government seems to benefit executive-legislative relations over foreign policy.

For one thing, politically difficult decisions require bipartisanship to ensure that not only one side bears the blame. Congressional scholar Thomas Mann explains, "Split party control of the two branches encourages an institutionalized partisanship, which often frustrates policymaking, but it also facilitates bargaining arrangements that diffuse political responsibility and allow each branch to avoid blame for unpopular but necessary policies."[54] Reflecting on his experience as director of the Congressional Budget Office from 1989 to 1995, Robert Reischauer makes a similar point: "I think there is one simple lesson that can be drawn from the recent experience. That lesson is that while united government may create the conditions under which budgetary gridlock can be overcome, it also can be politically destructive to the governing party. As such it is destabilizing."[55]

Divided government also forces the president toward the political center, where an internationalist foreign policy most naturally and comfortably resides. Divided government also forces the president to work harder on the substance of foreign policy and on explaining it to Congress and the public, since there can be little confidence that political arm-twisting will carry the day. Finally, because there is no expectation of a natural agenda-sharing that exists when the same party controls both branches, divided government seems to promote a greater willingness for participation and negotiation between the branches.

In the post–cold war era, U.S. foreign policy is threatened less sharply by divided government than by a growing ideological polarization in Congress that is undercutting the more centrist coalitions on which U.S. foreign policy has traditionally been based. Such ideological polarization is increasing the need for bipartisanship while simultaneously making such coalitions more difficult. When this ideological gulf is coupled with the deep divisions within both major national parties over many fundamental elements of foreign policy, it becomes clear that the fabric of political support for many aspects of foreign affairs has been torn in both directions.

Public and congressional support for the internationalist, free-trade-based foreign policy that has dominated U.S. foreign policy for the past fifty years is rooted in the center of the political spectrum. Liberal, pro-labor Democrats are no longer the sole repository of protectionist sentiments in Congress. Now they are joined by a number of Republican conservatives less committed to the free trade traditions of their forebears, creating an increasingly powerful coalition of extremes. To the extent that a moderate, bipartisan majority that cares about foreign policy remains, it is much more fluid and vulnerable to competing priorities and shifting currents than in the past. Even supporters of a moderate, pro-trade, pro-U.S. leadership foreign policy lack a fundamental consensus on core issues, such as U.S. policy toward Russia and China or the importance of arms control treaties, bringing into question their ability to sustain attacks from the minority. In the post–cold war era, with the possible exception of national missile defenses, very few foreign policy issues divide neatly along party lines.

More often, the far right and far left have joined forces to support more isolationist or protectionist policies, including more allied burdensharing, reduced foreign aid, and less free trade. In trade and international finance, foreign policy priorities such as funding for the IMF and fast-track trade negotiating authority have been stymied by similarly diverse coalitions.[56] This dynamic also plays an important role in congressional hostility toward China. Liberal human rights activists are now joined by religious conservatives concerned about the Chinese persecution of Christian minorities and national security hawks concerned about Chinese military activities. Pro-trade, business interests find themselves squeezed from both directions. Even the 1998 debate over NATO expansion demonstrated this "strange bedfellow" phenomenon. The nineteen senators who voted against expanding the NATO alliance to include Poland, Hungary, and the Czech Republic on April 30, 1998, included ten Democrats and nine Republicans and encompassed members from both ends of the political spectrum.[57]

The centrist nature of U.S. foreign policy and therefore its vulnerability to odd-couple alliances is not new. But with moderates on both sides of the aisle leaving in record numbers, Congress is more ideologically polarized than at any time since World War II. Congressional scholar Sarah Binder explains that in the 1960s and 1970s the "political center," defined as the combination of conservative Democrats and moderate Republicans, held steady at approximately 30 percent of Congress. By 1996 such "centrists" constituted only 11.3 percent of the House and just under 10 percent of the Senate. The ideological distance between Republicans and Democrats in both chambers of Congress has doubled since the late 1980s.[58] In this environment, defending a bipartisan internationalist foreign policy against ideological extremism is increasingly difficult.

Ideological polarization has widened the distance between Republicans and Democrats while failing to ameliorate fundamental disagreements within the parties over foreign policy. Today, both major parties face internal divisions over foreign policy fundamentals such as free trade, foreign aid, and America's role in the world, which limits their ability to influence members. Republicans are sharply divided over the general priority of foreign policy in the post–cold war world, the specifics of issues such as support for the United Nations, the importance of arms control treaties and foreign aid, and multilateral versus unilateral approaches to foreign policy crises. Increasingly, the probusiness and social activist wings of the party are squaring off over issues such as sanctions against religious persecution, funding for the IMF and international family planning, and free trade.[59]

Democrats face similar divisions over the priority of domestic versus foreign concerns, the role that the promotion of democracy, human rights, and conventional arms control should play in U.S. policy, and costs and benefits of free trade. Senator Pat Roberts (R-Kans.) has explained the situation in stark terms: "The internationalist wing of the Republican Party, once the bulwark of U.S. engagement abroad, is now barely represented on Capitol Hill. Meanwhile, Democrat members of Congress are becoming more and more protectionist over the excuse of losing jobs."[60]

Recently, the religious right has taken an increasingly vocal stand on various foreign policy issues, including international family planning, human rights and religious freedom, and even "normal trading relations" (NTR) status for China.[61] Such demands threaten to drive a wedge between many members of the foreign policy establishment and critical elements of their political constituencies. On the one hand, the centrist nature of U.S. foreign policy greatly complicates the ability to pass foreign policy legislation on a partisan basis. On the other hand, the moderate base, on which many of the central tenets of a traditional internationalist foreign policy depends, is increasingly unable to sustain a majority.

As a result, many recent legislative conflicts over foreign policy have involved battles within, rather than between, major political parties. For example, Senate ratification of the Chemical Weapons Convention betrayed deep divisions within the Republican Party. With Democrats united in support for the treaty, success or failure depended entirely on which wing of the Republican Party would control the debate. However, the NAFTA and fast-track debates displayed the open warfare between "free trade" and protectionist factions of the Democratic Party.

Because of these divisions, sustaining a united, party-based position on foreign policy legislation is extremely difficult, especially if the goal is to pass legislation rather than simply obstruct it. Take, for example, the 1998 efforts of Republican leadership to pass a State Department authorization bill, which would include support for U.S. arrears payments to the United Nations and other presidential priorities, as well as abortion-related funding restrictions on family planning organizations that was strongly opposed by the president. The House leadership had a hard time getting Republicans on board with the bill for a party line vote because so many of them did not want to provide *any* funds to the United Nations. Despite the Speaker's strong support, the measure had to be withdrawn once and then passed by the narrowest of margins because of opposition among House Republicans to any additional UN funding and Democratic opposition to the abortion-related provision.[62] After much arm-twisting, the Republicans passed a conference report signed only by Republicans that included controversial limitations on support for family planning organizations that perform or advocate abortions. In the Senate, the bill passed by only 51 to 49 because of the opposition to the abortion provision by moderate Republicans.[63]

Issue Leaders

As this chapter makes clear, congressional influence over foreign policy is a highly personal business. Institutions are important, but individuals drive the process. Who, however, are those individuals? The days when a few powerful committee chairs could dictate congressional behavior are long gone. Today, congressional leadership or influence on foreign policy derives less from traditional institutional roles or partisan loyalties and more from the personal drive and interest of any member who decides to champion an issue.

In both houses, foreign policy and national security are dominated by issue leaders, namely, champions and opponents for and against certain issues and policies. These leaders, and the staffers with whom they are closely associated, can play a powerful role by invoking the various tools at their disposal—investigations, floor speeches, holds, and so on—as well as driving the legislative agenda. Most members will defer to an issue leader as the institutional expert on a given issue and vote accordingly. Often, however, these issue leaders have developed such clout that their influence can be felt without ever resorting to the legislative process, especially on lower-profile issues. These members have grown adept at utilizing the informal sphere of influence, publicly and privately, to push their issues. Their opinions matter, and executive branch officials will take them into account or be prepared to suffer the consequences. Issue leaders can hold and benefit from important institutional positions, but these positions are not essential to their leadership roles.

Examples of this sort of independent, issue-based approach to foreign policy are everywhere. Senator Patrick Leahy (D-Vt.) has used his position on the Senate Appropriations Committee to lead his crusade against antipersonnel landmines. Senator Richard Lugar (R-Ind.) plays a major role on many foreign policy issues, particularly in arms control, even though he has not been chairman of the Senate Foreign Relations Committee since 1986. Representatives Nancy Pelosi (D-Calif.) and John Porter (R-Ill.) are passionate advocates of human rights issues. For many years Senator John Glenn waged war against the proliferation of weapons of mass destruction from his position on the Senate Governmental Affairs Committee. These members, and others like them, usually maintain an ongoing, sustained interest in these topics. They also have staffs who are committed to the issues and follow them closely should the members' attention be necessary.

In fact, given the rapid pace of events and the breadth of their responsibilities, members of Congress could not sustain such issue leadership without motivated and experienced staff. Since the early 1970s, the numbers and the experience levels of congressional staffers have expanded dramatically. As Hugh Heclo pointed out in 1978, "The new breed of congressional staffer is not a legislative crony or beneficiary of patronage favors. Personal loyalty to the congressman is still paramount, but the new-style legislative bureaucrat is likely to be someone skilled in dealing with certain complex policy issues, possibly with credentials as a policy analyst, but certainly an expert in using other experts and their networks."[64] Congressional staffers are now widely accepted as full-fledged foreign policy professionals, operating in a community of foreign policy elites. The growth of a professional staff in the legislative branch that clearly operates as part of the foreign policy establishment greatly facilitates the dynamic of issue leadership.

Christine DeGregorio has done innovative work on congressional issue leaders and confirms that while rank and institutional position are important factors in identifying congressional leaders, they are by no means sufficient. She interviewed 97 issue advocates who in turn identified those leaders inside the House of Representatives whom they found critical in guiding six major bills through the legislative process. These advocates identified 383 individuals as leaders, 36 percent of whom were professional staff. Interestingly, however, 9 out of 10 staffers identified as leaders operated in conjunction with an elected leader. In addition, most staffers specialized in certain fields.[65] She finds that "knowledge of the subject matter, experience in the chamber, a facility for bargaining and compromise, the right committee assignments, and commitment to hard work" figure prominently among the characteristics of congressional issue leaders.[66] This study concentrates on individuals who led high-profile legislation to completion, but nothing suggests that their role would be any less prominent in the informal arena.

Robert S. Gilmour and Eric Minkoff provide a case study involving the advance medium-range air-to-air missile (AMRAAM) weapons system that graphically demonstrates the power and influence of issue leaders in a fragmented and decentralized Congress. The U.S. Air Force began developing this weapons system designed for advanced air-to-air combat in the early 1970s. During the next fifteen years, as major cost overruns and technical failures mounted, the program became the subject of intense controversy and conflict between Congress and the U.S. Air Force and ultimately resulted in the sharp curtailment of the program. The authors demonstrate in detail, however, how the controversy was initiated and sustained by one House staffer and one member. Gilmour and Minkoff explain, "One senior House Armed Services Committee staff professional [Tony Battista], a congressman [Denny Smith (R-Ore.)] and his personal staff who were unassociated with the primary oversight committees for defense, and the GAO" were the primary instigators of congressional criticism of the AMRAAM system. Representative Smith had "no significant defense interests in his district, nor was he a member of either the Armed Services or Appropriations committees having jurisdiction over AMRAAM."[67] Representative Smith was a classic issue leader.

Individuals in Congress have always used informal and procedural tactics to influence specific foreign policy issues. As individualized and informal powers have grown in importance, however, issue leaders are playing an increasingly important role in the policy process. Moreover, there are several aspects of the post–cold war foreign policy environment that seem to contribute to the prevalence and importance of issue leaders. First, as mentioned earlier, the growing complexity of U.S. foreign policy is bringing more and more players from both branches of government into the foreign policy mix.

Second, for most foreign policy practitioners, the lack of political salience for and public interest in foreign policy is a double-edged sword. Experimenting with U.S. foreign policy no longer bears the risk of U.S.-Soviet nuclear confrontation. There may not be much interest in foreign policy, but unlike the situation during the cold war, neither is there much risk in trying to use foreign policy for political advantage. Moreover, the lack of political and institutional discipline gives members of Congress greater flexibility to act on issues they care about. Given that no compelling, overarching framework exists for U.S. foreign policy today, it is hardly surprising that policy entrepreneurship and single-issue advocacy seem to be on the rise.

Finally, disinterest on the part of the public (and a majority in Congress) gives a greater role to those members with a particular concern or issue. These members may emerge as issue leaders because they have the electoral confidence to engage in issues that interest them or because a certain issue appeals to an interest group or constituency of importance to the member. In this environment, individual members or staff with a particular foreign policy interest can have greater impact than ever. Says one Republican House staffer, "If a majority of members is uninterested in foreign policy, the members with well-shaped opinions will play a greater role."[68] Under these circumstances it is not surprising that the foreign policy issues that are prevailing on Capitol Hill today are those that appeal to a single-issue constituency.

Implications

It is common to hear policymakers in the executive branch bemoan the rise of partisanship and the intrusion of electoral politics into U.S. national security and foreign policy as they speak nostalgically of a time when politics stopped at the "water's edge."[69] Similarly, they yearn for united government—that is, having both Congress and the executive under the control of the same party—as if it were the "holy grail" of a disciplined and well-mannered foreign policy. These very desires, however, in some ways underscore how little many policymakers understand about how Congress and the executive really make foreign policy. In reality, the nation's political parties are deeply divided over foreign policy. Foreign policy priorities are buffeted by ideological extremism, and divided government has left a legacy of "institutionalized partisanship" that has exacerbated traditional institutional rivalries. Moreover, Congress has grown increasingly fragmented and its role in foreign policy increasingly individualized. Enhanced by various informal and procedural routines, these tendencies have contributed to the dominance of "issue leaders" over institutional "office holders" and issue loyalties over partisan allegiances.

What are the implications of this individualization and fragmentation for executive-legislative relations? First, the individualization of foreign policy in Congress has greatly complicated communication and consultation between the branches. Administration officials often must deal with a different cluster of members on almost every issue. The traditional phone calls to the leadership and committee chairs no longer guarantee that the key players have been addressed. Likewise congressional issue leaders face similar problems sorting out the myriad federal agencies and departments (not to mention the relevant subcomponents) that are involved in many foreign policy issues. This problem has probably grown more difficult since the end of the cold war because now even less agreement prevails on the relative priority of different issues, and there is little analytical structure to guide both branches of government to similar conclusions. This institutional fragmentation can lead to waste, duplication of effort, and poor coordination in both branches.

Growth in individual power favors congressional obstructionism, already a tremendous problem for perceptions of congressional credibility. Individual members cannot legislate alone, since it still takes a majority to pass legislation, but a single individual can often cause delay or defeat. As a result, Congress's ability to "construct" appears to have declined, while its ability to "obstruct" seems to have expanded significantly. In this unstructured setting, identifying and collaborating with an in-house champion is the only way to pass legislation. Without a champion, the executive faces an uphill battle in pursuit of any legislative initiative. However, one ardent opponent (especially in the Senate) can create nearly insurmountable roadblocks through the use of holds, filibusters, and other obstructive techniques.

These trends, when combined with the general disinterest on the part of the public and a majority in Congress, also have serious implications for the leadership and direction of U.S. foreign policy. Today, the interests and experience of the nation's elected officials increasingly reflect the public's disinterest in foreign affairs. In 1992, the first post–cold war national election, Americans elected their first "baby boomer" president, a man with little foreign policy background and no military experience. In Congress, most members in both the House and Senate have been elected since the end of the cold war, and for the first time, veterans are a minority in both Houses.[70] Moreover, in recent years, retirements by foreign policy leaders such as Sam Nunn, William Cohen, and Lee Hamilton have decimated the ranks of the internationalist "old guard." A national trend toward term limits may prevent the foreign policy confidence and experience of lawmakers from reaccumulating. As incumbents, members could develop expertise and experience in foreign affairs as they grew more confident of their electability. Today it seems far more difficult to develop the next generation of foreign policy leaders.

THREE   *Institutional Overlap and Issue Clusters*

At the formal, institutional level, relations between Congress and the executive over foreign policy are deeply adversarial. Beyond the glare of media attention and partisan hyperbole, however, Congress and the executive are neither as hostile nor as separate as they appear. Rather these institutions are linked together by long-standing personal ties, overriding issue loyalties, and bureaucratic self-interest. In this largely informal environment, collaboration and negotiation are as important to the formation of foreign policy as confrontation and conflict. Moreover, it is not uncommon for clusters of informal collaborators from Congress, the executive, and various nongovernmental entities to team up against similar "issue clusters" with opposing views. These complex and cross-cutting relationships define reality for most policymakers.

The notion that like-minded members of Congress, nongovernmental organizations, interest groups, and elements of the executive tend to form symbiotic, collaborative relationships on certain issues is not entirely new. The analysis of "subsystems" and "subgovernments" has been a staple of public policy literature and can provide some useful tools for explaining the fragmented and cross-cutting nature of executive and legislative relations as well as the complex and independent role of nongovernmental actors. This sort of analysis is also now used to explain the shifts in international relations that are minimizing the role of the "nation-state" as a unitary actor on the world stage.

Whether it is Douglass Cater's "iron triangles," Hugh Heclo's "issue networks," Paul Sabatier's "advocacy coalitions," or the "policy communities" and "policy networks" described by R.A.W. Rhodes, Steven Wilks, and Maurice Wright, public policy scholars have spent the past thirty-five years trying to understand and explain how governmental departments, congressional committees, and interest groups tend to step out of their institutional homes and come together to promote certain policies and seize control of particular issues.[1] Much of this literature is highly theoretical and emphasizes the dispersal of power away from the political (and electorally accountable) leadership and toward groups of executive bureaucrats, congressional staff, and lobbyists who may share certain self-interested goals. As a result, there tends to be a negative or undemocratic connotation to these groupings and associations.

Putting aside such negative connotations and broad theoretical conclusions, however, these concepts explain much about the way that Congress and the executive branch really make foreign policy. In practical terms, "issue clusters"—informal groupings of like-minded policymakers from Congress, the executive, and nongovernmental entities—are the key to understanding the day-to-day, behind-the-scenes reality of executive-legislative relations over foreign policy.[2] Issue clusters are not permanent, immovable structures; rather they can be short-lived or enduring, depending on the nature of the issue, the goals the participants hope to achieve, and longevity of the individuals involved. They can, and often do, incorporate the political as well as the bureaucratic layers of government and therefore are not necessarily undemocratic. Moreover, the positive or negative connotations associated with these issue clusters are more often based on whether individuals believe that their policy preferences are helped or hindered by the power of these relationships than from their mere existence.

Institutional Loyalties and the Prerogative Police

Our constitutional system expects each of the three branches of government to guard its constitutional prerogatives jealously.[3] Edward S. Corwin coined the now famous phrase describing the U.S. Constitution as "an invitation to struggle for the privilege of directing American foreign policy."[4] Such a struggle was predictable. The U.S. Constitution is deliberately ambiguous about the division of foreign policy responsibilities. The Constitution grants only Congress the power to declare war while installing the president with the responsibilities of commander in chief. The executive is charged with most diplomatic authorities, including the negotiation of treaties and international agreements, but the Senate must provide "advice and consent." The president may appoint his diplomatic team, but his ambassadors and other senior officials are subject to Senate confirmation. Finally, while the president commands the tremendous power of the executive bureaucracy, Congress holds the purse strings on all of his operating and programmatic expenses.[5]

These constitutional contradictions have created a system that is organically confrontational and naturally hostile, contributing to a deeply engrained sense of institutional loyalty in the bureaucracies of both branches. Describing this phenomenon, former assistant secretary of state for legislative affairs Douglas Bennett has noted that "the experience of the Carter administration suggests that partisanship does not bind the majority in Congress to the White House as much as the separation of powers separates them."[6]

Institutional loyalty is a powerful force. Throughout both branches of government, newcomers are schooled early, either formally or informally, on the preservation of their institutional rights and obligations by the "prerogative police" of their respective institutions. In most cases, the institution's lawyers are charged with this policing function. For example, it is usually up to the lawyers to vet all legislation to ensure that it does not infringe upon the prerogatives of their respective institutions. The secretary of defense's annual submission to Congress for the defense authorization bill routinely takes more than six months to proceed through the departmental and then interagency clearance processes, while all of the parties ensure that power and authority within the executive branch have not been altered or redistributed.[7] The prerogative police are even more vigilant in matters of presidential authority. Issues such as use of military force and war powers, command and control for U.S. peacekeepers, and funding cutoffs for military actions can provoke such broadly held institutional hostility that they are virtually unresolvable. Congressionally initiated legislation that seems to impinge on constitutional responsibilities of the president is quickly labeled "veto-bait."

Years of divided government have also exacerbated institutional conflict by permitting a commingling of the tools of partisan politics and institutional prerogative that has proved extremely difficult to disentangle.[8] Since 1968, divided government has become more the rule than the exception, producing a legacy of institutional hostility that bears partial responsibility for the state of executive-legislative relations today. Many of the congressional staffers who joined the Clinton administration in

1993 were shocked to be on the receiving end of this deeply engrained hostility. As one official who made this move explained, "One day we were colleagues and the next day it was 'us' and 'them.' It was amazing how quickly the change occurred. They certainly didn't want to do something for us just because we asked."[9]

Sometimes institutional loyalties are used to mask policy differences. As a result, it is not uncommon for members of Congress to complain about procedures and prerogatives ("we were not consulted" or "Congress must authorize") when the real disagreement is over substance. Even if a majority in Congress cannot agree on a policy direction, there is almost always a majority to fight for "institutional rights." Similarly the executive branch will lambaste Congress for meddling and micromanagement, when the real battle is over policy preferences. Congressional concerns about the Clinton administration's policy toward Bosnia, and more recently Kosovo, have often fallen into this dynamic.

In fact, war powers and use of force issues seem particularly vulnerable to this commingling of institutional and partisan loyalties. Members and staff who join the executive branch often seem to have a change of heart about war powers and the requirements of congressional approval once they have found themselves on the other side of the issue. In Congress, Democrats used to lead the charge in support of war powers and the role of Congress in authorizing military action. Yet when the Clinton administration took over, early plans to solve the "war powers" problems with a more conciliatory approach toward Congress were quickly shelved. With a Democrat in the White House and Republicans in control of Congress, the tables have now turned, with Republicans such as Representative Tom Campbell (R-Calif.) leading the fight for congressional authorization of U.S. military operations in Kosovo.[10]

Collaboration, Cooperation, and the Spillover Effect

An excessive focus on institutional conflict over foreign policy, however, can lead to what James Lindsay describes as the "adversarial fallacy," namely, a "preoccupation with the conflictual side of executive-legislative relations."[11] In fact, the institutional rivalry that characterizes much of the formal and public discourse between the branches belies the extraordinary informal collaboration and cooperation that occurs at all levels of the government. Huge quantities of information move through these informal, backdoor channels every day. Many of these working relationships can precede and outlast a given administration. Without them, U.S. foreign policy could descend into total gridlock over the most routine issues. Given the cumbersome nature of the formal legislative process, it is hardly surprising that the informal methods of solving problems become so attractive.

Often, these channels allow both sides to get the information necessary to diffuse a situation before it develops into a crisis. Moreover, in an environment where conflict lies more precisely between issue leaders than institutions, collaboration with a congressional champion is essential to any executive-legislative strategy. While this backdoor communication and cooperation is essential for resolving many problems, it can sow the seeds of conflict and controversy by transferring executive branch disagreements into the congressional arena. Nothing exemplifies the complexity of executive-legislative relations over foreign policy more than this "spillover effect," namely, the extent to which congressional concerns with or opposition to administration policy resembles, or even originates from, interagency disagreements.

By accident or design, the substantive disagreements between Congress and the president over foreign policy often mirror the arguments and battles of the interagency process. In part, spillover is a natural outgrowth of genuine policy disagreements. Given that policy decisions always involve different viewpoints and difficult trade-offs, clear-cut uncontroversial answers are the exception rather than the rule. On a tough issue, the interagency process can mean months of weighing options, airing viewpoints, building consensus, and escalating difficult decisions for higher-level review—and that is when it is working well. There is no greater unanimity in Congress on controversial foreign policy issues than elsewhere in the foreign policy community. It is natural, then, that the same substantive concerns and trade-offs should surface within Congress.

Inevitably, when elements of the bureaucracy disagree with decisions taken by their own senior leadership or another agency they use these informal channels to share this perspective with their congressional counterparts. As one Department of Defense official explains, "Nobody in this town gives up any more because there is always somewhere else to go to get another day in court."[12] In fact, these relationships help to discipline the interagency process and temper disagreement by providing a course of action for the disaffected. That same official continues, "Informal backdoor relationships force the institutions to operate more effectively and efficiently because they are scared of the back door . . . the backdoor process is hugely effective in keeping things honest and running no matter how much we hate it."[13] In other words, the knowledge that elements of the bureaucracy always have an opportunity to take their grievances elsewhere forces the executive branch to try to resolve differences and reach consensus. Of course any disgruntled participant can still try to find a sympathetic ear for his grievances, but they are likely to be more isolated if most of the interagency players seem to be in agreement.

Process as Predictor

A perception that the interagency process was relatively thorough and fair always helps to smooth the way with Congress. The quality and character of the interagency process are often a very good predictor of congressional response. The more contentious the issue is within the executive, the more contentious it will be on the Hill. The spillover problem intensifies when an ineffective or heavy-handed interagency process leaves participants feeling frustrated and marginalized or when there is too much pressure to make contentious decisions appear unanimous.

In 1993 and 1994 the Clinton administration tried to push through a major overhaul of U.S. peacekeeping policy, including a plan to shift a large portion of UN peacekeeping assessments to the Department of Defense. The proposals fell victim to a bitter interagency process, while events on the ground in Somalia, Bosnia, and elsewhere were raising questions about the overall direction of U.S. peacekeeping policy. The Department of Defense (particularly the military services) objected to a number of the proposals, particularly the funding, which seemed to treat the department as a "cash cow." The sense was that the Clinton administration was transferring many inappropriate funding responsibilities into the Defense Department because that was the only place they could get the funding. The Defense Department and its oversight committees were concerned about this diversion of resources, especially if the department did not retain full authority and responsibility over how the funds were spent. The State Department, while interested in finding additional resources, felt that some of the proposals trampled the traditional prerogatives of the secretary of state and risked eroding the influence and power of the State Department.[14]

As interagency negotiations deadlocked, the controversy quickly spilled over to Congress as elements from both departments tried to use their congressional contacts to sway the debate and shore up their positions. Such aggressive sharing of "dirty laundry," however, also fed into growing apprehensions among members about peacekeeping and the United Nations. Meanwhile, the administration's legislative advisers were rejecting congressional requests for consultations on the new peacekeeping policy because the funding issues had not yet been resolved. Jeremy Rosner explains, "Ultimately, the *funding* problem would sabotage the administration's relations with Congress on peace-keeping *policy*."[15] Both the defense and foreign affairs oversight com-mittees rejected the new policies and funding proposals. It took another year for the interagency to produce a sharply scaled down peacekeeping policy in the form of Presidential Decision Directive 25. By that time congressional opposition to peacekeeping and the United Nations had solidified, and any form of Defense Department funding for UN peace-keeping was rejected for yet a third time.[16]

The way that the administration portrays the decisionmaking process and acknowledges internal disagreements can also make a difference. Attempts by the executive to stifle disagreement and represent difficult and controversial issues as unanimous decisions usually do not work and often backfire by increasing congressional skepticism and prompt-ing concerns that Congress is not getting the full story. Says Michael Van Dusen, former staff director of the House International Relations Committee, "All of the tough decisions in the executive branch are 55-45 decisions, often pitting one group or agency against another. . . . I understand that the administration feels a lot of pressure to get its ducks in a row before testing a decision either overseas or domestically . . . but it is hard to portray the complicated and combative executive process as a 95-5 decision."[17] Under these circumstances congressional staffers will usually look for the real story and more often than not, they will find someone willing to tell it to them.

Several interviewed officials (in both branches of government) referred to the annual drug certification process for Mexico and other Latin American nations as a classic and frustrating example of this dynamic. Under a 1986 antidrug law, the president must certify that countries receiving U.S. assistance are fully cooperating with U.S. coun-ternarcotics efforts. Without the certification, sanctions prohibiting non-humanitarian assistance go into effect unless the president chooses to "waive" the requirement. The certification process always produces a nasty battle within the executive branch, often pitting the Department of Justice against the Department of State and the Department of Defense.

The national security adviser sends a recommendation to the president for a decision and then sends all the disagreeing parties to Capitol Hill to explain the decision as a "united front." The ruse never fools anyone.[18]

Leveraging: Congressional Influence and Executive Reactions

If issue-based, cross-institutional alliances explain how these "separate" institutions are so deeply intertwined, they do not fully explain why. Once again the way that Congress influences policy is critical. As described in chapter 2, Congress influences foreign policy through a variety of formal and informal devices. These techniques not only help to disperse power but also create issue-based linkages or issue clusters. Many of the informal techniques that members and their staffs use to influence policy involve leveraging executive branch behavior rather than legislating policy directly.

Leveraging can occur privately and informally as members of Congress and their staffs take advantage of personal contacts and relationships to voice concerns and raise issues. It also occurs publicly as members make effective use of the media and the "bully pulpit" of their office. Whether on the floor of the House or Senate, in committee hearings, on the Sunday morning talk shows, or on the op-ed pages of the nation's leading newspapers, these members have ample opportunity to lead public opinion and guide the foreign policy establishment, all in an attempt to influence executive decisionmaking. In fact, representatives from both branches use the media to convey positions and test approaches not only with the public but also with one another. Says Jeremy Rosner, former senior director for legislative affairs at the National Security Council, "The morning and weekend talk shows become an almost daily colloquy between members of Congress and the administration as each side frames its argument and floats trial balloons for consideration by the other branch."[19]

Why is the executive branch responsive to leveraging? The executive is under considerable pressure to predict and accommodate congressional concerns to prevent conflict escalation or collateral damage. Despite their institutional rivalries, policymakers and legislators also share a common interest in identifying and resolving differences informally. Whenever possible, senior members of the executive will go to great lengths to accommodate fellow establishment members in the Congress through such means as briefings, phone calls, and delays.

There are several reasons for this accommodating posture. First, by handling issues quietly and informally, both sides can prevent the issue from escalating and preserve valuable working relationships. Often, executive branch officials want to work an issue out quietly to prevent a member of Congress from taking an issue "public" where the debate is less nuanced and the executive branch has less maneuverability than an individual congressman or senator. Human rights issues often provide classic examples of this dynamic. Public castigation of countries such as Indonesia, China, or Turkey can have painful reverberations in bilateral relations that many executive branch officials would prefer to avoid. Besides, no one wants to be "against" human rights. It is a public relations game that is very hard for the president to win; therefore, congressional human rights activists have far greater flexibility to advocate their position. In addition, once the issue has moved to the public arena, officials in both branches have less room for flexibility and negotiation without appearing to have backed down in front of political allies and constituents. A win-win solution is much easier to come by in the informal universe.

Sometimes the reasons are more personal. As one insider explains, "There is so much revolving door between the staffs of the executive and legislative branches" that there is often a vested interest to avoid conflict, especially at the most senior levels.[20] And many of President Clinton's senior foreign policy advisers, including Secretary of Defense William Cohen, National Security Adviser Samuel Berger, Secretary of State Madeleine Albright, and Director of Central Intelligence George Tenet, are former members of Congress or served at some point in their career as congressional staff. These relationships can create an incentive to try to minimize conflict, at least on a personal level.

The AMRAAM case mentioned in the previous chapter vividly illustrates this kind of public leveraging. House staffer Tony Battista used his extensive contacts in the Defense establishment to uncover serious problems in AMRAAM performance and underreporting of cost overruns. Representative Smith first tried to use more informal avenues through his personal contacts to influence the process. When informal contacts failed to produce a sufficient response by the Defense Department, the congressman changed course and began a letter-writing campaign coupled with "an increasingly successful press conference and media strategy." [21] As Robert Gilmour and Eric Minkoff explain,

Smith's numerous letters and widely reported statements created a good deal of angst in the AMRAAM program office and they received careful attention in the Office of the Secretary of the Air Force. Each letter, coming and going, had to be considered as both a policy event and a press event. The Air Force response, in the view of Smith and his staff, was to 'stonewall us' . . . Smith knew of these omissions because of his own expertise in the area and because he too had 'moles' inside the Pentagon. As often as not, he had the relevant data and answers even before the Air Force briefed him.[22]

The executive branch also fears—with justification —retribution if it ignores congressional requests and inquiries. "Fencing" (making the expenditure of funds subject to restriction, reporting, or notification) or cutting funding, additional reporting requirements, hostage-taking (linking the resolution of one issue to another unrelated matter), and other obstacles often result when more informal expressions of congressional will are ignored. In the first year of the Clinton administration, Representative David Obey (D-Wisc.) (then chairman of the Subcommittee on Foreign Operations, Export Financing and Related Programs of the House Appropriations Committee), got wind of Defense Department plans to fund exchange programs and training activities with friendly foreign militaries out of the Defense Department budget. Obey's staff felt this military-to-military "contacts" program bore strong resemblance to the International Military Education and Training program (IMET), which is part of the foreign assistance budget and subject to the jurisdiction of the international operations subcommittee.

Angered by the perception that the Defense Department would circumvent his jurisdiction to augment military assistance, Obey cut funding for IMET in half even though the defense funding was never appropriated. It took several years for IMET to rebound to its previous funding level despite the strong support of the chairman of the joint chiefs and all of the regional commanders in chief. The message was received. Today, everyone treats the IMET program, which is much beloved and coveted by senior military and defense officials, with kid gloves.

When informal pressures are not successful, congressional members and staffs will often seek to legislate their way into the executive decisionmaking process, by introducing procedural steps like reports, notifications, and certifications designed to force the executive to keep Congress in the loop or by creating a more sympathetic bureaucracy. Through a vast array of laws, members and staff force the executive to invite Congress deeper into the decisionmaking process than might otherwise be the case. Reports, notifications, and certifications force the executive to engage in more transparent decisionmaking and give members numerous opportunities to ferret out problems, force decisions, and elevate concerns. U.S. arms transfer policy, an area of traditionally high congressional interest, is riddled with procedural requirements and multilayered notifications. Furthermore, much of the legislation passed between 1994 and 1996, which requires routine consultations with Congress on peacekeeping operations, provides a classic example of how Congress can use prenotifications and consultations to limit and observe executive behavior.[23] Such procedural legislation is often embedded in broader legislation and addressed through quiet negotiation with the executive. These provisions are rarely subject to broad scrutiny, let alone a vote by the entire body. They certainly get less public attention than the more dramatic policy gestures, but they create tremendous anxiety within the executive bureaucracy.

Congress also has the "ability to mandate structures and procedures [that] can give members of Congress a way to build their preferences into the policy-making process without having to pass substantive legislation that specifies how the United States will relate to other countries."[24] Congress has effectively used this approach to direct bureaucratic and organizational attention to key policy areas by creating an executive bureaucracy that is more sympathetic to congressional concerns. Through much of the 1970s and 1980s the trend was toward the creation of new executive offices to focus on congressional priorities. The Arms Control and Disarmament Agency, the State Department's Bureau of South Asian Affairs, and the Defense Department's Office for Special Operations and Low Intensity Conflict are among the many executive offices that were established by congressional directive. G. Calvin Mackenzie writes how the congressionally mandated Bureau of Human Rights and Humanitarian Affairs (reorganized in 1994 and renamed the Bureau of Democracy, Human Rights, and Labor) often enjoys "better relations with Congress than with its counterparts" in the State Department because "the bureau's philosophy more closely aligns with the views of its congressional creators than with the prevailing routines, incentives and policies in the diplomatic corps."[25] This is a tendency that is often replicated in other congressionally mandated elements of the federal bureaucracy.

In the 1990s, Congress has also used legislation to pare back the bureaucracy and shrink executive resources. For the past several years, the House National Security Committee has supported legislation designed to shrink the Office of the Secretary of Defense and return organizational power to the military services. Mandatory personnel cuts and bureaucratic restructuring have had a major impact on the departmental decisionmaking process and the balance of power among the services, the joint staff, and the Office of the Secretary of Defense. Similarly, Jesse Helms has made reorganization of the foreign affairs bureaucracy a hallmark of his chairmanship. Conflict with the executive branch over the reorganization and consolidation of the foreign affairs agency dominated the Senate Foreign Relations Committee for over three years and at several points brought other committee business to a complete halt.[26]

Even substantive foreign policy legislation is intended more often to influence the executive in its policy choices than to direct policy or coerce the behavior of foreign officials. G. Calvin MacKenzie describes Congress's ability to cut off foreign aid as "a kind of club behind the door. . . . Knowing that Congress has the ultimate power to cut off aid, the executive branch will often work more aggressively to bring about changes in the country in question or accept conditions that Congress seeks to impose on the provision of aid."[27] The executive branch will negotiate quietly with Hill staffers, often conceding on policy or funding, to prevent the sanction from coming into effect. The legislation "brings the executive to the table" with Congress.[28] Many staffers also believe that congressional mandates can help the executive to take on difficult issues like human rights if "they can place the blame on Congress," through a sort of "good cop, bad cop" routine.[29]

The impact of these informal and procedural actions can be hard to quantify, but it is real in terms of behavior modification, additional consultations, and escalation of the decisionmaking process within the executive. Often executive branch officials will attempt to forecast congressional concerns and inoculate proposals against likely difficulties, something the literature refers to as "anticipated reactions."[30] By making modifications to policies and proposals in light of expected congressional opposition, the executive branch can facilitate a more favorable congressional response. These reactions, however, can be very deleterious to the policy process when an element of the executive feels compelled to distort the facts in an effort to sustain congressional support.

This seems to have happened with the U.S. Air Force advance medium-range air-to-air missile weapons system (AMRAAM) program. According to Robert Gilmour and Eric Minkoff, "Air force anticipation of negative congressional reactions to realistic estimates of AMRAAM development needs contributed to the service's over-optimism and deceit with regard to technical problem solving cost projections."[31]

In other cases the reaction is more benign, although not necessarily more beneficial for policy. For example, when the Clinton administration proposed the Warsaw Initiative, a plan to provide $100 million in military assistance to countries participating in the Partnership for Peace, it deliberately accounted for congressional concerns in the very construction of the proposal. The administration, hoping to keep the jurisdictional squabbles that had plagued its early efforts at a minimum, divided funding for the program between the State Department and the Defense Department according to existing authorities (legislative provisions already on the books) and areas of responsibility. As a result, the executive requested $60 million for the program as part of the State Department's foreign military financing budget. The defense budget included $40 million for joint exercises and training with partner countries.

This approach allowed the administration to keep a low profile on the program, avoid any jurisdictional squabbles between the foreign affairs and defense committees, and dispute the argument that defense resources were being used for nondefense purposes. With this simplified proposal, both the State Department and the Defense Department could argue that the program did not represent a significant departure from "business as usual" for either department. There were, however, significant policy drawbacks. First, despite attempts to increase the State Department's overall budget to account for this new funding requirement, Congress funded the program while significantly cutting the department's overall budget top line. As a result, the Warsaw Initiative was funded at the expense of other Department of State programs and priorities. Second, by operating under existing authorities, the Department of Defense had very little flexibility in the use of its funds for the program and had to struggle to develop a coherent plan to use all of the funds effectively.[32]

Senior officials in the State Department and the Defense Department were persuaded that the improved prospects of congressional support were worth the policy and programmatic risks. The approach proved successful. Congress fully funded the $100 million as requested for fiscal year 1996 and continued to do so in 1997, 1998, and 1999. The decision to split the funding and use only existing authorities did have serious downsides in terms of policy distortions, management difficulties, and limited flexibility. In the views of most officials involved, however, this was an acceptable price to pay for maintaining congressional support and securing the overall funding.

Interest Groups and Issue Clusters

Few aspects of executive-legislative relations are more controversial and misunderstood by the foreign policy community than the role of special interests and other nongovernmental entities in the foreign policymaking process. Many foreign policy experts, including many in the executive branch, tend to assume that interest groups affect policy indirectly by exerting influence, primarily over Congress, in an effort to tip the executive-legislative scales. Since, so the thinking goes, congressional action on foreign policy is "tainted" by the excessive influence of special interests and requirements of electioneering, Congress is almost incapable of behaving responsibly on matters of foreign policy.[33] In reality, this approach overstates electoral politics as the principal motivation of congressional action on foreign policy, oversimplifies the complex relationship between members of Congress and so-called special interests, and obscures and distorts the substantive, independent, and sometimes constructive role that interest groups and ethnic constituencies play in U.S. foreign policy.

Interest groups can play a much more direct and independent, and sometimes more significant, role in U.S. foreign policy than as simple manipulators of congressional behavior. As explained earlier, elements of Congress and the executive tend to form cross-institutional linkages that form the basis for both collaboration and spillover. Executive-legislative relations do not occur in a closed system. Rather, interest groups, ethnic constituencies, and other nongovernmental entities tend to participate in these issue clusters. In today's more open system, interest groups are not simply "influence peddlers." Rather these issue advocates gravitate to congressional issue leaders and participate in highly collaborative relationships with elements of both branches. As Christine DeGregorio explains, "Advocates need accommodating leaders to interject their points into the formal decision-making process. And the legislators need information, brokers, and confidants to help them assemble enough votes for passage."[34] It is not uncommon for these nongovernmental entities to team up with elements of one or both branches of government to advocate certain foreign policy positions, with each of the participants performing different, yet critical, functions.

Interest groups often serve an informal liaison function between the two branches of government, acting as "water-carriers" between Congress and the executive branch when more direct dialogue is awkward or prohibited. Hugh Heclo noted this development in his 1978 essay on issue networks, saying, "Within government, the operation of issue networks may have a second advantage in that they link Congress and the executive branch in ways that political parties no longer can."[35] This means of communication is particularly important when more direct contacts between the branches are tightly constrained by restrictive policies or when relations are strained. In interviews, several officials from both branches mentioned the way nongovernmental entities served this function, sometimes going so far as to act as an informal "honest broker" between the branches by airing compromises and legislative "fixes" with both sides.

For example, arms control organizations have often played this "water-carrier" role in support of the Cooperative Threat Reduction program. This Defense Department program, often called the Nunn-Lugar program for its congressional sponsors, Senators Sam Nunn and Richard Lugar, assists the states of the former Soviet Union with the safe destruction and dismantling of their strategic nuclear weapons and forces. Despite its congressional origins, the program's annual authorizations and appropriations have often come under challenge, particularly in the House. Often, nongovernmental organizations such as the Arms Control Association and Business Executives for National Security have played a critical role in responding to congressional opposition and providing information. As one official with long experience with the program explains, "What we had was an indirect alliance between the administration and the Senate, mediated by arms control NGOs, to address the concerns of the House staff."[36]

For obvious reasons, interest groups naturally gravitate toward issue leaders, simultaneously benefiting from and augmenting the individual power of these members. Whether it is Representative Nancy Pelosi's close working relationship with the human rights community or Senator Leahy's efforts with the International Committee to Ban Landmines, the effect is the same. When those relationships exist, these groups become an important source of data, information, and advice. They also function as an early warning system of what may be happening in other parts of the government or even in other capitals. Similarly, these organizations know that they can count on these members to champion their cause and represent their interests. General public disinterest in foreign policy gives many members a lot of latitude to pursue particular foreign policy interests without fear of political backlash, even if their views do not correspond with mainstream America or even with their own constituents.

Many of these organizations are even emerging as significant nongovernmental actors on the world's foreign policy stage. In some cases, their impact may have less to do with the amount of political pressure they can bring to bear on a given candidate (traditional function of interest groups) and more to do with the way they are seeking to fill the leadership vacuum themselves by engaging in very public campaigns to articulate a policy vision. The International Campaign to Ban Landmines is a classic example of how information technology and global communications are empowering international interest groups. Operating on a shoestring budget, this ad hoc coalition of more than 1,000 organizations in 60 countries was a driving force behind the December 1997 signing of the Convention on the Prohibition on the Use, Stockpiling, Production and Transfer of Antipersonnel Mines and on Their Destruction, by 121 countries.[37] Despite the strong opposition of the Clinton administration and particularly the U.S. military (the United States has not signed the treaty), this ad hoc coalition of individuals and organizations often collaborated with antilandmine issue leaders in Congress, such as Senator Patrick Leahy (D-Vt.).[38] The coalition's impact was so profound that in 1997 it was awarded the Nobel Peace Prize. In her Nobel acceptance speech, Jody Williams, campaign coordinator, singled out Senator Leahy for his leadership on the issue.[39]

In a 1997 *Foreign Affairs* article, "Power Shift," Jessica Mathews describes the dramatic growth in nongovernmental organizations whose resources and expertise often outstrip that available through the public sector. Propelled by the power of the Internet and other forms of low-cost communications, transnational nongovernmental networks are offering "unprecedented channels of influence." As Mathews explains, "Women's and human rights groups in many developing countries have linked up with more experienced, better funded, and more powerful groups in Europe and the United States. The latter work the global media and lobby their own governments to pressure leaders in developing countries, creating a circle of influence that is accelerating change in many parts of the world."[40] Margaret Keck and Kathryn Sikkink describe this phenomenon as the "boomerang pattern."[41]

No longer are these organizations and networks limited to operating through governments, as in a traditional interest, or pressure, group. Their activities are not even confined to participation in domestic "issue clusters." Rather, these organizations increasingly have the ability to strike out on their own, to dominate rather than just influence policy. Jessica Mathews describes how at the Earth summit in Rio de Janeiro in 1992, nongovernmental organizations and their representatives set the agenda, served on delegations and otherwise "penetrated deeply into official decision-making."[42]Admittedly, nongovernmental organizations cannot have this much influence across the policy spectrum, but that they are having it at all has tremendous implications for executive-legislative relations and foreign policy. Both branches of government are dependent on the public awareness, information-gathering, and liaison functions these nongovernmental entities provide. Nongovernmental organizations are more often calling the shots rather than following them.

Issue-based Policy

By cultivating relationships with clusters of like-minded congressional issue leaders, these groups easily fall into step with the single-issue advocacy that is prevalent in Congress now. Issue clusters care about issues—landmines, religious persecution, arms control, nonproliferation, human rights, and various ethnic interests—just to name a few. In many ways this "issue-based policy" favors Congress over the executive branch. Members of Congress have an ability to concentrate on one foreign policy issue to the exclusion of others that the executive branch simply does not share. Without a countervailing or balancing force, however, this fractured, issue-based approach to foreign policy can have disastrous consequences, as efforts in one arena tend to have unintended consequences elsewhere.

The increasing use of sanctions legislation in the 1990s demonstrates how issue-based policy can have a splintering effect on foreign policy. Thomas Daschle (D-S.D.), Senate minority leader, has noted, "The United States has imposed economic sanctions 115 times since World War I—and 61 times since 1993."[43] The proliferation of sanctions is not part of an overarching plan or strategy to expand their use; rather they represent a "tangle of good intentions"—support for holocaust survivors, human rights, nonproliferation, religious persecution, and so on—with the unintended consequence of tying U.S. foreign policy up in knots.[44] As different clusters of government officials, congressional staff, interest groups and even state and local governments search for leverage on their issue, sanctions are often one of the only options available to demonstrate their efforts. Given the dramatic decline in U.S. foreign aid since the end of the cold war, members of Congress have few alternatives for pressuring the behavior of foreign governments, as well as the executive branch. As members of Congress search for a vehicle to affect policy, sanctions provide one of the few options that lie within the legislative domain.[45]

Ironically, dramatic reductions in foreign aid mean that the leveraging power of sanctions, especially unilateral sanctions, is very limited. Notes one seasoned observer of Congress, "Congress has been spending less on foreign assistance and relying more on sanctions as if these are policy alternatives. In fact, they cancel each other out."[46] It seems likely that the diminishing utility of unilateral sanctions clearly figured into the Indian and Pakistani calculations as to the costs and benefits of testing nuclear weapons.

In this problem, however, also lies the solution. The diminishing utility and increasingly problematic consequences of sanctions legislation has helped to ignite a sanctions backlash in the Congress.[47] Spearheaded by a highly organized industry consortium called USA Engage, think tanks, farm interests, industry officials, executive branch officials, and even some prominent members of Congress have started a steady drumbeat of opposition to the use of sanctions, especially unilateral and or secondary sanctions, as a "painless" foreign policy option. In just a couple of years the antisanctions movement has gained enough ground that sanctions supporters are feeling the need to fight back. In a 1999 article for *Foreign Affairs*, Senator Jesse Helms declares, "The distortions spread by this small cabal of lobbyists in the name of American business are inexcusable."[48] Although by no means eliminating congressional enthusiasm for sanctions, this countervailing issue cluster is providing a much-needed check on the excessive use of sanctions in a manner that is flexible and highly responsive.

Implications

Congress and the executive branch are porous, permeable institutions, rife with cross-institutional linkages and often operating in an obscure, informal universe of influence. Institutional divisions are often horizontal as well as vertical. Moreover, these institutions do not operate in a closed system. Rather, the legislative and executive branches of government "cohabitate," often as part of issue clusters with interest groups, ethnic constituencies, and other nongovernmental entities that hope to influence the direction of U.S. foreign policy. Information technology—fax, e-mail, the Internet —allows cluster members to be in nearly constant communication. Loyalties are complex and conflicting, as policymakers in both branches often find their institutional allegiances and responsibilities in conflict with their policy preferences. As a result, it is not surprising that the formal, public relationship between the branches differs significantly from the informal, private relationships of their many subcomponents.

Moreover, sanctions are not the only "tangle of good intentions" in U.S foreign policy today. Today's issue-based foreign policy creates similar tangles complete with the accompanying internal inconsistencies and unintended consequences. The *à la carte* nature of today's foreign policy makes it increasingly difficult to sustain support for a coherent and integrated vision for the future, especially within Congress. Without the emergence of new unifying principles for U.S. foreign policy, single-issue constituencies, spearheaded by increasingly effective interest groups, are likely to multiply. Communications technology, especially the Internet, is making issue advocacy cheaper, easier, and more flexible. Meanwhile, cuts in staff and personnel and support agencies, along with general bureaucratic inflexibility, will increasingly limit the ability of either branch of government to generate and distribute information independently and thereby compete with the nongovernmental sector.

The speed and accessibility of modern information technology also almost guarantees that such independent organizations will become increasingly important. The ability of these interest groups to target the executive and legislative branches as well as media outlets, opinion leaders, and the general public quickly and independently overwhelms the capabilities of the government and ensures that in the future few big issues will be decided solely by the "insiders." In today's environment, major initiatives that do not involve close coordination with interest groups and nongovernmental entities are almost destined to failure. Both Congress and the executive branch need these groups to build support, provide sustained media attention, and secure endorsements.

FOUR   *Three Turkish*
        Frigates

IN 1995 THE U.S. Navy decided to offer three frigates that it no longer needed in its own inventory to the Turkish military. What began as a seemingly simple, noncontroversial request to give Turkey three excess U.S. ships became in the end a major thorn in U.S.-Turkish relations and a fairly serious point of tension between Congress and the executive branch. No one could have imagined that it would take almost three years to win final congressional approval for the transfer of these three ships and that the controversy would come to dominate U.S.-Turkish relations at even the highest levels of government. The story of these three ships is a classic example of how individualized power and informal influence can drive many day-to-day foreign policy issues between Congress and the executive branch.

The dispute over the Turkish frigates resulted almost entirely from the informal influence of powerful issue leaders working in concert with sympathetic elements of the bureaucracy and like-minded interest groups. The issue was never debated on the House or Senate floor, and the controversy never really surfaced in the mainstream media. Though the transfer required legislative approval in its earlier stages, after early 1996 the president faced no legal impediment to transferring the ships. It was informal agreements and routines that kept the ships at dock until mutually acceptable arrangements could be negotiated—a powerful demonstration of the informal universe at work.

Early Turf Battles Cause Delay

In early 1995, the U.S. Navy reached an agreement with its Turkish counterpart to transfer three U.S. frigates to Turkey. The frigates were seen as a way to cement relations with the Turkish Navy, reward the Turks for their support of key U.S. policies, and encourage the Turks to purchase follow-on American-made equipment. Turkey would pick up all the costs of transferring the ships and training the new crews, and the U.S. Navy would save the decommissioning and storage costs.

Since the ships were valued at approximately $60 million dollars each, the transfer required explicit congressional authorization. The U.S. Navy submitted what it thought would be a noncontroversial request for these three ships as well as five other ship transfers to Egypt and the Persian Gulf. The navy's request included a total of seven ships to be provided on a grant basis and one on a lease basis.[1] The navy considered the ships critical to regional defense cooperation activities and pursued the request aggressively. Since the navy was already planning to decommission the ships, it felt it could do a good deed while saving the decommissioning and storage costs it would otherwise incur by mothballing the ships. Navy officials estimated that it would cost about $10 million to decommission the ships and $1 million a year to store them.[2] As excess defense articles, these ships could be transferred to Turkey at little or no additional cost to the U.S. Navy. To keep costs down, however, the navy needed to transfer the ships "hot," namely, before the decommissioning process had started.[3]

The request initially encountered little trouble in the Senate, which included the requested legislation in the Senate version of the fiscal year 1996 Defense Department authorization bill, but the plan hit a firestorm in the House. There were two main problems. First, the proposal fell into a bitter congressional jurisdictional squabble. While the Senate gave jurisdiction for the transfers to the Senate Armed Services Committee, the House gave jurisdiction for the issue to the House International Relations Committee. Unless the committee provided advance approval, the House National Security Committee, now the House Armed Services Committee, could not include the transfers in its markup without exposing the defense bill to a possible sequential referral to the other House committee. Sequential referrals ensure that all committees have an opportunity to review legislation involving issues under their jurisdiction, but the process is lengthy and cumbersome and can introduce much delay into the legislative process.

In any case, the House International Relations Committee was not inclined to acquiesce easily. It saw the navy's request and use of the Defense Department bill as a deliberate attempt to avoid the committee's jurisdiction over the grant transfers and responded angrily. The turf battle spilled back into the executive branch as the State Department, Defense Security Assistance Agency, Department of the Navy, and the Office of the Secretary of Defense argued over approach and strategy on behalf of their congressional oversight committees.[4]

Several members of the House International Relations Committee and their staffs strongly opposed the large number of grant transfers in the packages, which they considered excessive "foreign aid" to wealthy Persian Gulf countries (Oman, United Arab Emirates, and Bahrain) or countries that already receive sufficient military assistance (Egypt and Turkey). In short, they saw the navy's "giveaway" program as an inappropriate augmentation of foreign aid.[5] Speaking to *Defense News* on the issue, Representative Sam Brownback (R-Kans.) explained, "We have to send a strong message that we cannot be a sugar daddy to the world. . . . We are broke."[6]

The House committee dug in its heels and made clear that it would not support the seven grant transfers, at the same time complaining bitterly about the process to the State Department and the Defense Security Assistance Agency. The House National Security Committee announced that it would defer to the House International Relations Committee on the issue. The navy's initial instinct was to try to push through the request by weighing in at higher and higher levels. The navy was convinced that it had a lot riding on these ships because of its relationships with these key regional allies. The increased pressure, however, had the unintended effect of making the Senate Armed Services Committee more attached to its version of the legislation while solidifying the opposition from the House International Relations Committee. As the issue escalated, it became clear that compromise would be necessary. Deciding which countries would get their grants "withdrawn" became an intense debate within and among the Office of the Secretary of Defense, the State Department, and the Department of the Navy. They finally agreed to transfer four ships by grant and four ships by lease or sale. Turkey would get two of the grants and one of the leases.[7]

The reworked package of leases and grants was then incorporated into the fiscal year 1996 Defense Authorization Act with little added controversy. The conferees did impose new requirements that any repair and refurbishment be done at a U.S. shipyard, and they added limitations on future grant transfers.[8] Although the ship transfers were resolved, the overall bill became caught up in a major battle with the administration over unrelated issues, including missile defenses. As the fight dragged on, the navy and the Turks were increasingly concerned that the "hot" transfer might not be possible and that costs for Turkey would climb. Those fears were exacerbated when, for unrelated reasons involving missile defenses, the president vetoed the first version of the defense authorization bill. It was not until February 10, 1996, that the fiscal year 1996 Defense Department authorization bill was finally signed and the ship transfers authorized to begin.

In reality, however, this legislative authorization was only the beginning of the congressional approval process, since the ships were still subject to the Foreign Assistance Act (FAA) and Arms Export Control Act (AECA) notification processes. In fact, three separate notifications would be required, one for the grant transfers, one for the lease, and one for the sale of necessary munitions and Defense Department support.[9] Forecasting just such a problem, the navy had tried to include a waiver of FAA and AECA notification requirements in its original legislative proposal. That suggestion had prompted another turf problem in the Senate where jurisdiction over the transfers went to the Senate Armed Services Committee, but any revision to the FAA or AECA automatically went to the Senate Foreign Relations Committee. The armed services committee had no choice but to drop the waiver. Members and staff of the Senate Foreign Relations Committee and House International Relations Committee knew that they would get another chance to weigh in before the transfers were complete.[10]

Conflict Erupts

Meanwhile events in the eastern Mediterranean were making matters worse in Washington. In January 1996, Greece and Turkey barely averted conflict over an uninhabited island in the Aegean. The Imia-Kardak dispute reignited concerns about Turkish-Greek relations and the balance of power in the Aegean, especially within Congress. Despite Turkey's strategic importance, congressional support for Turkey is very fragile. Propelled by ethnic Greek-American interests, several members are very concerned with regional instability and the balance of power in the Aegean, that is, the Greece-Turkey dynamic. Turkey is also often under attack by the human rights contingent in Congress, especially because of its treatment of Armenian and Kurdish minorities in the region. Without much of an ethnic constituency of its own, Turkey's supporters tend to be concentrated on the armed services committees, whose members are more sympathetic to Turkey's role as a strategic ally and more sensitive to Turkey's importance as a major importer of defense goods and services.

The ink was barely dry on the authorizing legislation when the State Department got the word that the foreign affairs committees, because of the tensions in the Aegean, would not look favorably on the transfers at that time. Consistent with longstanding practice in the face of such a recommendation, the State Department withheld the necessary notifications, hoping the climate would improve for congressional support of the transfer.[11]

On March 29, 1996, President Clinton met with Turkish President Süleyman Demirel, who complained bitterly about the delay on the frigates. Upon conclusion of the meeting, the president directed that the notifications be sent immediately. The State Department was in a quandary. March 29 was the last day before an extended congressional recess and by long-standing agreement, the State Department did not forward arms transfer notifications on the eve of a recess without prior coordination with the committee staffs. The president's decision left the State Department with little choice, so it forwarded the two thirty-day notifications on the grants and the lease, withheld the fifteen-day notification on the support package, and hoped for the best.[12]

The Power of Congressional Holds

Unfortunately, much as the State Department's legislative advisers had expected, the notifications angered the committee staffers. On April 3, House International Relations Chairman Gilman and ranking Democrat Lee Hamilton wrote to complain about the recess notification and put the transfers on hold.[13] To make its point, the House committee offered to release the ships on May 15, not inconsequentially thirty days after Congress returned from recess. Before the administration could accept the offer, Senator Paul Sarbanes (D-Md.) contacted National Security

Adviser Anthony Lake and asked for a delay. Senator Sarbanes felt that tensions in the Aegean were still too high for the transfer to proceed. At the end of April, a letter from Senator Pell, ranking minority member of the Senate Foreign Relations Committee, on behalf of Senator Sarbanes cited concerns about the balance of power between Greece and Turkey and heightened tensions in the Aegean and requested that the ships be withheld indefinitely. Gilman decided to defer to Senator Sarbanes and supported an indefinite hold.[14]

Once the notifications expired at the end of April, there was no legal impediment to the transfers. To prohibit the transaction, Congress would have had to enact a resolution to stop the transfers with enough votes to override a presidential veto. Long-standing practice and painful lessons learned, however, made the administration very reluctant to ignore a hold, especially one conveyed in writing by a member. As one congressional staffer explains, "Failure to respect the hold could trigger all-out warfare on foreign policy between the executive and the Congress . . . It would have been a bridge burner from which the administration could never have recovered."[15] Interventions by the secretary of state, the national security adviser, and other senior officials to try to get Senator Sarbanes to withdraw the hold did little to loosen his resolve. It seemed to accomplish just the opposite, as Senator Sarbanes stiffened his position and repeatedly urged the administration to direct its attention toward the Turks instead of him.[16]

Reportedly the president discussed the matter with Senator Sarbanes in the spring of 1996 but made no progress. Further attempts to get the president to engage Sarbanes on the issue seemed to go nowhere.[17] The standstill fueled rumors in some quarters that the president was resistant to putting significant pressure on Senator Sarbanes, or in fact to overruling him by releasing the ships, because of the senator's role on the committee investigating Whitewater.[18] It is difficult to prove or disprove such an accusation, but a politically charged explanation is not necessary for anyone who understands the power of the informal "hold" system over the executive branch, Senator Sarbanes's long-standing views on these issues, and the significance of his tough stance to his constituents. One need not look to Whitewater to explain why the president would not be eager to arm-twist a prominent Democrat whose support he needs on numerous other foreign policy issues, let alone various domestic and personal ones. The State Department certainly had an interest in avoiding antagonizing their oversight committees and a key senator whose support it needed on a host of other issues. Staffers on both sides of the Hill stressed their expectation that any administration would have observed the "hold" rather than risk the punitive action that releasing the ships would certainly have triggered.

The Pressure Builds

As the controversy continued, the frigates became a major irritant in U.S. bilateral relations with Turkey, with the Turks threatening to withhold cooperation on various strategic issues, such as supporting U.S. operations in Iraq. Concerned about the hostile congressional climate on both the Greece-Turkey and the human rights fronts, the State Department stopped forwarding all major Turkish arms transfer notifications to Congress, prompting the Turks to accuse the United States of imposing an "informal embargo" against one of its closest allies.[19] Meanwhile, the lengthy delays kept driving up the price tag for the frigates. As the dispute dragged on through the summer, Turkey had to recall hundreds of naval personnel who were in the United States for training to take over the ships and bring them back to Turkey at a cost of almost $40 million. In August of 1996, the navy had to transfer the ships to "modified safe stowage" status (a middle ground between a "hot" ship and a fully mothballed one). Reactivating the ships would now cost the Turks an additional $5 million.[20]

In November 1996 Turkey, increasingly frustrated, threatened and ultimately canceled plans to buy ten Super Cobra attack helicopters (a sale valued at $150 million). The order eventually went to Eurocopter.[21] Admittedly, the Turks knew that several elements in Congress opposed the helicopter sale on human rights grounds and that it was unclear if the sale would ever have been approved. Pro-Greek lobbyists, arms control and human rights organizations, and even Armenian interest groups were well organized in opposition to the sale. Senator Sarbanes along with twenty other senators signed a letter to the president opposing the sale.[22] Nevertheless, Turkey's public gesture of frustration did convey a message to the administration and stirred concerns in the arms industry. Turkey then threatened to shut U.S. companies out of the competition for a coproduction agreement to build 145 attack helicopters worth $3 billion.[23] Industry pressure to resolve the impasse built steadily, but Senator Sarbanes remained unmoved, reiterating his objections to the frigate transfer in a February 19, 1997, letter to the president.[24]

In that letter, Senator Sarbanes suggested that "an agreement by both sides to renounce the use of force or the threat of force in their bilateral relations, to respect the principle of sovereignty and territorial integrity, to abide by international law, to pursue dialogue and good neighborly relations, and to identify appropriate mechanisms for crisis prevention and dispute resolution, would be a reasonable and constructive step."[25] The proposal in the senator's letter mirrored the text of a proposed agreement sponsored by the European Council and supported by Greece, but not Turkey, in July of 1996. Declared a Sarbanes staffer, "We made it clear to the administration repeatedly that lifting the hold would be very difficult unless both Greece and Turkey agreed to these principles."[26] Administration sources confirm that the senator's staff had been circulating the text of the proposed European Council statement and suggesting it as the basis for resolving the impasse since the summer of 1996.

For the better part of a year, however, this approach did not go anywhere. First, getting such an agreement was not as easy as it might appear, given Turkey's firmly entrenched policy of opposing "conditions" on its assistance from the United States. Lower-level attempts at getting such an agreement were repeatedly rebuffed. In April of 1997, U.S. officials tried to negotiate a "nonaggression pact" based on these principles, but discussions broke down without an agreement. In addition, executive branch assumptions about the nature of Senator Sarbanes's motivations served to limit the range of options that were seriously considered. The assumption was that this was a political problem, which required a political solution (or political arm-twisting). Such cynicism made more substantive approaches seem like a waste of time.

On April 18, 1997, three top aerospace executives sent a letter to President Clinton appealing for an end to the de facto embargo. A month later, Turkey announced that it would not "give a single new defense contract to U.S. firms . . . until the United States releases the transfer of three frigates it had pledged to deliver."[27] While it is not clear that the industry pressure was having much effect on Senator Sarbanes or Chairman Gilman, other members such as Senator Strom Thurmond (R-S.C.) and Senator Jesse Helms (R-N.C.) were definitely starting to feel the heat. In June 1997, Senator Helms threatened to put holds on three destroyers destined for Greece until the Turkish ships were released. The Greek military, upon realizing that they would also be affected, suddenly found the impasse less appealing and reflected that understanding in discussions with Capitol Hill and the administration.[28]

Breakthrough

Opinions on whether or not the counterhold by Helms on the Greek ships was the deciding factor vary dramatically, and somewhat predictably, among various congressional staffers. Once other key senators began to take a strong interest, especially those in the majority, and the "hostage-taking" among "pro-Greece" and "pro-Turkey" members began to escalate, Senator Sarbanes's hold became more and more unsustainable. It is also clear, however, that such political pressure was not sufficient to break the impasse or it would have done so. As one Senate Foreign Relations Committee staffer described the situation, "The administration seemed to fundamentally misunderstand Senator Sarbanes's motivations and intentions regarding the frigates from day one. They did not take him at his word that there were substantive issues involved, instead assuming that his position was motivated by anti-Turkish sentiments that could only be resolved through political pressure."[29]

While not everyone involved is convinced of the purity of the senator's motives, there is no question that once he had committed himself publicly against the frigates, he would need a substantive basis to change course. In addition, several officials in the State Department and the Defense Department acknowledge that the issue had become a "matter of principle with Sarbanes" and efforts to "roll" him were utterly ineffective.[30]

Meanwhile, the stakes for the administration were rising on a bilateral and regional level, and pressure to resolve the issue was enormous. Following consultations with key staffers, Pete Petrihos, then deputy director of the Office of Southern European Affairs at the State Department, resurrected the idea of a joint statement, this time tied to the NATO summit in Madrid. Secretary of State Madeleine Albright agreed to work the issue as a side bar to the summit, which was focused primarily on NATO expansion. The new initiative had several benefits. First, the new Turkish election had brought new players into the mix who might be more amenable to an agreement. Second, with the Greek president and the Turkish prime minister both attending with their foreign ministers, the Madrid summit offered an opportunity to cut a deal at the highest level. Third, this initiative focused narrowly on mutual agreement to a simple statement that could be read by U.S. officials rather than a formal pact or accord.

The initiative was handled very quietly, but State Department officials shared their ideas with both the Greek and Turkish foreign ministries and with Senator Sarbanes's staff.[31] On July 9, 1997, on the margins of the NATO summit meetings, U.S. Deputy Spokesman James B. Foley announced that "the Turkish and Greek Ministers reached a convergence of views on a basis for promoting better relations." This agreement was based on a set of principles that were almost identical to the July 1996 European Council proposed statement.[32]

This fairly modest step at regional cooperation seemed to provide the substantive basis that Senator Sarbanes and Chairman Gilman wanted to end the stalemate and lift the hold, which occurred almost immediately. In late July 1997, the Department of Defense, through the Defense Security Assistance Agency, submitted the required notifications to Congress, stressing that the transaction would not "adversely affect either the military balance in the region or U.S. efforts to encourage a negotiated settlement of the Cyprus question."[33] The thirty-day renotification of the transfer expired at the end of August 1997, and the ships were on their way to Turkey by early 1998, arriving almost three years after they were initially promised.

Implications

The Turkish frigates provide a powerful demonstration of the way that policy gets made in the ocean. These ships were the subject of behind-the-scenes jockeying for almost three years. Although the fate of the three ships became a major irritant in U.S.-Turkish relations—a disagreement serious enough to engage both the Turkish and American presidents—the conflict barely emerged in the mainstream press, covered only by defense industry publications and regional media. Starting in April 1996, the president faced no legal restriction on the transfer of the three frigates to Turkey, yet the ships sat for another year and a half after that date because of the power of a single senator and the force of long-standing informal arrangements. This episode would not show up in any statistical analyses of voting patterns because no votes were ever taken, but its policy impact was significant.

On matters involving conflicts in the Aegean and relationships between Greece and Turkey, Senator Sarbanes is a classic issue leader. The administration had to work the issue out with him personally. His leadership derives more from interest, experience, and motivation than from his institutional position. He was neither the chairman nor the ranking minority member of the committee, although his presence on the committee was clearly advantageous.

It is easy to brand this issue leader-issue cluster dynamic as a simple function of traditional "ethnic politics." Such simple electoral motivations, however, are inadequate. Senator Sarbanes's Greek heritage, strong advocacy of Greece in the foreign aid process, and his views on the balance of power in the Aegean have earned him a prominent place in the Greek-American community and a reputation among some elements of the foreign policy community as a "captive" to Greek-American interest groups. The question is, to what extent can his views and actions be attributed to electoral politics? The answer—less than expected. As a four-term senator consistently elected by a wide margin, his political vulnerability is questionable. The senator is a popular incumbent. This position affords him the opportunity to focus on foreign policy issues that interest him. Moreover, most of his views on Greece and Turkey are deeply and personally held.

Electoral pressures from the Greek-American community do not conflict with the senator's own substantive calculations, and it is unlikely that the senator would ever pay a price for his positions on these issues from the rest of his constituents who do not care about foreign policy. As this case points out, it is often hard to tell if the "community" is leading the member or if the member is leading the "community." On the opposing side of the frigates issue, the increasing frustration of American business interests, particularly defense contractors, certainly captured the attention of other members and intensified the pressure on Senator Sarbanes but was insufficient to bring about a resolution. Even so, special interest organizations on both sides of the issues (primarily defense industry and Greek-American lobbyists) provided early warning and information to like-minded officials in both branches, making full use of the issue cluster dynamic.

In this case, these issue leaders derived their individual power almost exclusively from the use of an informal, administrative "hold." The Turkish frigates dramatically illustrate the pervasiveness and power of such administrative holds and how this system can be used by members of both the House and the Senate. Senator Sarbanes and Chairman Gilman used this system to stop the transfer of three frigates to Turkey, sometimes for procedural reasons and sometimes for substantive ones. Once the ships had been authorized and the requisite notifications had been sent, the president had no formal, legal impediment to releasing the ships. Nevertheless, the fear of retaliation was so great that the administration observed the holds for more than a year and a half, even though the hold was not legally binding and the delay in sending the frigates was undermining U.S.-Turkish relations.

Most legislative advisers agreed that the risk of subsequent legislation, punitive funding cuts, and a general lack of support by key committee members on other important issues demanded that the hold be observed. Especially in the eyes of the State Department and its oversight committees, the administrative hold system is nearly sacrosanct. No one interviewed for this study could recall a time that a hold had been blatantly disregarded since the system was first established in the mid-1970s. Moreover, it is not clear that such an attempt by the president would have made any difference. It could have backfired by angering these key members and further escalating the disagreement. Similarly, the House and Senate leadership showed little interest in stepping in and getting involved. It is unclear what, aside from counterholds and hostage taking, they could have done anyway. Sarbanes and Gilman had to be persuaded rather than overruled.

Once again, this case demonstrates how issue loyalties often seem to outweigh partisan ties, especially when the visibility on the issue is relatively low. A Democratic senator, Republican House member, and Greek-American interest groups joined together to oppose a Democratic administration, a few members of the armed services committees, and a broad array of arms suppliers. The Democratic senator at the center of the crisis was largely unmoved by fairly extensive pressure from fellow Democrats in the executive branch. Since the senator was "leveraging" the executive branch through the use of procedural agreements that were not highly visible, and he was supporting the president on other higher-profile issues, the disagreement was easily sustained. Senator Sarbanes's use of individual power and procedural leverage over the executive to force a policy shift demonstrated his skill as a master of the informal universe. The administration failed to play the game as well, antagonizing the committee staffers by prompting jurisdictional squabbles and failing to observe the appropriate notification rituals.

Spillover was a problem in the early stages of the legislative approval process. When it became clear that the House would not approve all of the ships on a "grant" basis, interagency and interdepartmental bickering over which countries would get the grants quickly spilled into the congressional committees, intensifying the disagreements between the House International Relations Committee, the House National Security Committee, and the Senate Armed Services Committee. Once again, informal collaboration and negotiation between the branches were the keys to resolving the controversy. A constant exchange of briefers and background papers from all parts of the executive branch kept information flowing among the key players. Finally, Pete Petrihos's role as interlocutor between the senator's staff and the executive branch eventually paved the way for a solution to the impasse.

The episode also reveals much about the cross-institutional relationships between executive departments and agencies and their respective oversight committees. The Defense Department was most anxious to get the issue resolved, and its oversight committees were sympathetic. Not sympathetic enough, however, to sour their own relationships with another committee. The State Department, however, was loath to antagonize a senator whose assistance it needed on so many other issues and therefore was inclined to let the issue drift without resolution. By the time the White House got involved and began to work the issue more directly, the situation had deteriorated a great deal, making it very difficult for either party to back down.

Political pressure on Senator Sarbanes largely backfired as the senator felt compelled to prove that he would not bend his principles to White House political pressure. The executive branch failed to develop a consistent or well-coordinated strategy for dealing with the issue. Defense officials became extremely frustrated and kept trying to put more and more political pressure on the senator. The State Department, particularly its legislative advisers, was nervous about antagonizing an important committee member and upsetting its informal system for arms transfer notifications. Hoping to limit provocations, State also sought to channel access to Senator Sarbanes's office through its legislative affairs branch, thereby limiting constructive efforts at informal problem solving. It was not until the State Department opened these lines of communication and found a formulation to allow all parties to "win" that the controversy was resolved.

If the executive branch had used the informal universe more effectively earlier on, much of this conflict could have been mitigated. More thorough interagency vetting and consultation with congressional staff probably would have turned up the concerns over the grant transfers and greatly facilitated initial authorization. Earlier authorization might have avoided the rest of the crisis. Failing that, working levels should have addressed the issue more aggressively and substantively in early 1996 in the context of the Imia-Kardak incident. Instead, the problem drifted until the Turks tried to force a solution directly with the president, prompting a sudden, poorly timed notification that further inflamed congressional concerns. Finally, participants waited too long to search for a substantive solution to the impasse that would allow all of the key players to walk away as winners. Zero-sum politics is a tough way to get results.

FIVE

Pakistan,
Proliferation, and the
Brown Amendment

IN EARLY 1995 THE Clinton administration joined forces with Senator Hank Brown (R-Colo.) in a determined effort to amend U.S. sanctions legislation prohibiting U.S. assistance and military sales to Pakistan. These sanctions had been in effect since October 1990 when the United States terminated assistance to Pakistan because President George Bush could no longer certify to Congress that "Pakistan does not possess a nuclear explosive device and that the proposed U.S. assistance program will significantly reduce the risk that Pakistan will possess a nuclear device."[1] These certifications regarding Pakistan's nuclear program are required by section 620E of the Foreign Assistance Act, a provision commonly referred to as the Pressler amendment. Between 1990 and early 1995, Hill watchers, staffers, and legislative experts of various stripes were united in their assessment that any attempt to modify or repeal sanctions legislation regarding Pakistan would fail and, worse yet, could backfire by provoking key members of Congress into taking even more punitive action. Yet by early 1996, the president had signed into law new language releasing more than $300 million worth of previously withheld military equipment and reopening some military and economic assistance to Pakistan.

The story of this legislation, commonly referred to as the Brown amendment in honor of its principal sponsor Senator Hank Brown, has both ocean and wave characteristics. On the one hand, the battle over the Brown amendment did not trigger significant public interest or media attention until very late in the process. More important, the controversy never acquired the characteristics of institutional or partisan conflict. It remained, for the most part, a battle among foreign policy professionals over the direction of U.S. foreign policy. The issue, however, did not lack for controversy or confrontation. Competing, bipartisan issue clusters fought vigorously in support of and in opposition to modifying the Pressler amendment. Strong issue leaders, working with nongovernmental organizations and sympathetic elements of the executive branch, made extensive use of individual powers and informal procedures to support and oppose sanctions relief.

On the other hand, the administration required substantive legislation to modify the existing law, something that cannot be accomplished strictly in the informal universe. Senator Brown had to make use of his institutional position and his individual powers to drive this provision through the legislative process, including a fairly high-profile, hotly contested vote on the Senate floor. While the Brown amendment did not accomplish all that the Pakistanis or the president desired, it did constitute a significant legislative victory for Pakistan, its supporters in Congress, and the Clinton administration. This case offers many valuable lessons on how Congress and the executive branch can use informal powers and powerful individuals to pass foreign policy legislation.

Origins of the Pressler Amendment

It is difficult to understand the significance of the Brown amendment without some background on the legislation it sought to modify, namely, the Pressler amendment.[2] In the late 1970s concerns about the Pakistani nuclear program prompted the Carter administration to curb U.S. assistance to Pakistan sharply. Such a step was required by U.S. nonproliferation legislation—primarily the Glenn and Symington amendments, which imposed sanctions on countries participating in the unsafeguarded transfer of nuclear-related technology.[3]

The Soviet invasion of Afghanistan, however, altered the equation, prompting the Reagan administration to request a large buildup in U.S. military and economic assistance to Pakistan. Between 1982 and 1990 the United States provided more than $6 billion in military sales and grant assistance to Pakistan, making Pakistan one of the top recipients of U.S. foreign aid.[4] Despite a fairly strong consensus on the role of Pakistan in countering Soviet expansionism in South Asia, expanded assistance to Pakistan did not come without controversy. The six-year assistance package approved in 1981 required a special waiver of the Symington amendment, which engendered significant debate in the House and the Senate.[5]

Despite this burst of military cooperation, deep-seated concerns in Congress about Pakistan's nonproliferation record persisted and grew. Several members of Congress, led by Senator John Glenn (D-Ohio), were increasingly resistant to the waivers and special exemptions of U.S. nonproliferation laws, which allowed this assistance to proceed. In 1985 Congress passed the Pressler amendment, named for its sponsor, Senator Larry Pressler (R-S.D.), which allowed Pakistan's special status to continue provided the president could certify that Pakistan did not possess a nuclear device. The provision could not be waived if the president could not make the necessary certification.

At the time, the amendment seemed a small sacrifice for continued assistance to Pakistan. Senator Pressler's amendment was a "second degree" amendment that had been negotiated with the administration as a substitute for a harsher version sponsored by Senator Alan Cranston (D-Calif.) (which had an impossible certification requirement). The Reagan administration viewed Pressler's version as the "lesser of two evils" and supported it as the price it had to pay to get assistance to Pakistan approved in light of concerns about the country's proliferation record.[6] Based on Pakistani assurances, the administration assumed that the sanctions would never be invoked. As one knowledgeable official explained, "With the Symington waiver and the Pressler amendment in place, the United States tacitly permitted Pakistan to retain the enrichment technology without sanctions going into effect, so long as it did not take the next step—actually producing a nuclear explosive device."[7]

Tensions again surfaced in 1987 when the Reagan administration requested another $4 billion in U.S. assistance for Pakistan, coupled with another multiyear waiver of the Glenn-Symington amendment. Fueled by additional disclosures about the Pakistani nuclear program, congressional nonproliferationists again raised concerns.[8] At the same time, however, the war in Afghanistan was reaching a critical junction, and many members were afraid that curtailing U.S. assistance to Pakistan could threaten the war effort. Finally, Congress approved a two-year extension of the waiver, but only because key Democrats—Representative Stephen Solarz (D-N.Y.) and Lee Hamilton (D-Ind.) in the House and Christopher Dodd (D-Conn.) and John F. Kerry (D-Mass.) in the Senate—defected to join most Republican members on key committee votes in support of a two-year waiver.[9]

In 1989, against a backdrop of rising suspicion about Pakistan's proliferation activities, newly elected Pakistani Prime Minister Benazir Bhutto visited Washington and spoke to a joint session of Congress. She pledged that Pakistan neither had nor would develop nuclear weapons.[10] During her visit, the prime minister formally requested seventy-one additional F-16 fighter aircraft. Later that year, Pakistan signed two contracts with General Dynamics to purchase eleven F-16s with U.S.-provided grants and loans, and a second, valued at $1.4 billion, to purchase sixty F-16s with Pakistani national funds.[11]

Sanctions Invoked

As the Soviet Union withdrew from Afghanistan and ultimately collapsed, congressional "nonproliferationists" held sway in the annual debates over aid to Pakistan. By October 1990, faced with growing evidence about the Pakistani nuclear program, President George Bush could no longer make the certifications required by the Pressler amendment, and assistance came to a sudden halt. No future contracts could be signed, and all of the equipment already in the pipeline was placed on hold. Besides the F-16 fighter aircraft (the first ones were then under construction), this equipment included three U.S. Navy P-3C military aircraft, 28 Harpoon surface-to-surface missiles, 360 AIM-9L "sidewinder" air-to-air missiles and other assorted minor items and spare parts.[12]

The Pakistanis, hoping that the situation could be resolved, continued to meet the payment schedule for the F-16 until 1994 even as the prospects for transferring the planes dimmed. In July 1994, Benazir Bhutto's second government reversed the policy of Nawaz Sharif and decided to stop payments. After renegotiating the contract with General Dynamics, it was decided that General Dynamics would build the maximum number of aircraft possible—twenty-eight—with the $658 million that had been paid to that date by Pakistan. These twenty-eight aircraft, after rolling off General Dynamics's Fort Worth assembly line between 1992 and December 1994, were then flown to Davis-Monthan U. S. Air Force Base in Tucson, Arizona, where they were stored at Pakistan's expense.[13]

By the time the Clinton administration took over in 1993, bilateral relations with Pakistan were badly frayed as a result of the standoff. Debate raged in the administration over how to break the impasse. The "nonproliferationists," particularly those at the Arms Control and Dis-

armament Agency, felt that the administration should only make concessions in exchange for concrete results on the Pakistani nuclear issue. The
regionalists, particularly in the State Department's Bureau of South Asian
Affairs and the Department of Defense, argued for a more "multifac-
eted" approach to U.S. policy toward Pakistan that would allow greater
cooperation in the areas of drugs, terrorism, peacekeeping, and military
training. While the regionalist perspective prevailed in the administration, the nonproliferationists, led by Senator Glenn and Senator Pressler,
were stronger in Congress. In the House, although Representative Lee
Hamilton was sympathetic to Pakistan, Representative Benjamin Gilman
and several key staffers on the House International Relations Committee
strongly supported the Pressler amendment. Each of the camps enjoyed
strong networks both between branches and with ethnic and arms control interest groups, including the Pakistani and Indian embassies and
their professional lobbyists, all of whom followed the debate closely.

Efforts to Resolve the Impasse

The issue first came to a head in 1993 when the Clinton administration
decided to submit to Congress a broad rewrite of the Foreign Assistance
Act. In late 1993 and early 1994, following repeated crises in Haiti,
Somalia, Bosnia, and elsewhere, relations between the Clinton administration and Congress were at a particularly low ebb. The redrafted act
was widely seen by members and staff as an attempt by the executive
branch to reduce, or at least challenge, the role of Congress in foreign
affairs. It was not well received.[14]

The rewrite process had been highly acrimonious even within the
executive branch, and many issues quickly spilled over onto the Hill.
One of the last issues to be resolved in the interagency process was
whether or how to include the Pressler amendment in the administration's proposed legislation to Congress. Elements in the executive
branch differed strongly over the policy implications of eliminating the
provision as well as over the likely congressional reaction. In the end,
the administration decided not to include the Pressler language, thereby
avoiding all country-specific references in the bill. In accompanying letters and statements, however, the administration tried to assure Congress that "even if a new foreign assistance act without specific language
on Pakistan were passed, we would continue to apply Pressler standards
to Pakistan."[15]

Those assurances, however, were not enough to quell a strong congressional reaction, forcing the administration to backtrack. In a February 3, 1994, news conference, Agency for International Development Administrator J. Brian Atwood said, "We heard the Congress loudly and clearly on that . . . and we've decided to retain the Pressler amendment as well as the Glenn-Symington amendment."[16] The revised FAA was never passed; however, the administration's proposal prompted such a firestorm in Congress that by 1994 the Pressler amendment was widely perceived as a congressional sacred cow. Many legislative advisers insisted that any further attempts to repeal or modify the Pressler language could risk a serious congressional backlash. By all accounts, the Pressler amendment had become symbolic of Congress's place at the vanguard of nonproliferation policy, and Senator Pressler, who originally sponsored the amendment to "help" the executive fend off more onerous legislation, had become, along with Senator Glenn, one of its most ardent champions.

The administration next tried a diplomatic initiative to trade the stored F-16s for a verifiable cap on the Pakistani nuclear program.[17] Such a plan would require a special congressional exemption to permit planes to be released. Senator Glenn expressed strong opposition to the plan, and Senator Pressler vowed to "do everything in [his] power" to block the deal. [18] Working closely with key nonproliferation and arms control interest groups, as well as sympathetic elements of the executive branch, Senators Pressler and Glenn provided formidable opposition to any sanctions relief. Before it even got to Congress, however, the plan was bitterly rebuffed by the Indians and the Pakistanis. As one official explains, "The Pakistanis would not bargain away their security for twenty-eight aircraft and the Indians believed that any initiative that could bolster Pakistan's defenses was a threat to their security."[19] Another official recalled, "The foundation of the proposal was nothing but balsa wood; it was destined for failure."[20] Once again the administration went back to the drawing board.[21]

By 1995 U.S. relations with Pakistan, an important regional ally, were becoming more problematic. Complaints about the "unfairness" of U.S. policy pervaded every facet of U.S. foreign policy with Pakistan. Besides feeling "singled out" by the Pressler sanctions, which dealt only with Pakistan, the Pakistanis deeply resented that the United States would return neither the planes and other equipment covered by the sanctions nor the money (more than $650 million) that Pakistan had paid for them. Moreover, the U.S. government was "charging" Pakistan for storage costs for airplanes they could not have. Resentment over this perceived unfairness was so widely held in Pakistan that any concession to the United States on the issue was considered politically unsustainable.[22] In the Clinton administration discontent with this "hamstrung" policy toward Pakistan was growing and so was sympathy for the "keep the money or the planes, but not both" argument. Cooperation on key areas such as terrorism, peacekeeping, and counternarcotics had become more and more difficult, while U.S. legal restraints seemed to have little or no effect on the proliferation problem.

Perry Goes to India and Pakistan

In January 1995 Secretary of Defense William Perry traveled to Pakistan and met with Pakistani officials who pressed their case for a repeal of the Pressler amendment. Perry, while expressing skepticism that Congress would grant such a wish, succeeded in reestablishing regular, high-level military discussions with his Pakistani counterparts.[23] Shortly after his return, on January 31, 1995, Secretary Perry made a speech before the Foreign Policy Association in which he began to make the case that the Pressler restrictions were counterproductive to U.S. nonproliferation goals and debilitating to U.S.-Pakistani relations. Secretary Perry, describing the depths of Pakistani frustrations over the Pressler amendment said, "I've never been to a country where even the taxicab drivers and the school children know in detail about a law passed by the U.S. Congress."[24]

With the April visit of Pakistan's Prime Minister Benazir Bhutto bearing down, the administration again took on the question of legislative relief for Pakistan but made little headway on the substance or tactics of the proposal. Legislative advisers in the State Department, the Department of Defense, and the White House continued to express skepticism that the Pressler amendment could be modified, much less repealed. Many advisers assumed that the proposal would be a nonstarter with Congress, so most of the responses to the president's request for proposals were very modest. Disappointed with their timidity, senior officials rejected these initial proposals.

Shifting Ground on Capitol Hill

Meanwhile, however, the ground was shifting on Capitol Hill. With the Republican takeover of Congress in November 1994, Senator Hank

Brown assumed the chairmanship of the Subcommittee on Near Eastern and South Asian Affairs of the Senate Foreign Relations Committee. Trying to find a way to improve the situation with Pakistan was a priority for the committee staff and the administration. Early on, Senator Brown proved sympathetic to improving U.S.-Pakistani relations and began a series of private discussions with Secretary of Defense Perry, Assistant Secretary of State for South Asian Affairs Robin Raphel, and others in the administration on how to address the situation.[25] Now sanctions relief had an issue leader to provide a critical counterweight to Senators Glenn and Pressler. Moreover, prosanctions relief elements in the executive, as well as the private sector, now had a "go to" person in the Senate.

Senator Brown took ownership of the issue and decided to shepherd the initiative through the legislative process. Senator Brown came to view the proposal as one of his "legacy items" and was determined to see the issue through before his retirement at the end of the session. Senator Brown's "tenacious personality" proved well suited to the task at hand.[26] Suddenly sanctions relief had a champion prepared to go head-to-head with Senators Glenn and Pressler. The legislative landscape had changed dramatically.

On March 9, 1995, Senator Brown chaired a hearing, "Nuclear Proliferation in South Asia," with the clear intention of beginning the debate over changing the Pressler amendment. While stopping short of specific details, the administration representatives at the hearing, Robin Raphel, assistant secretary of state for South Asian affairs; Joseph Nye, assistant secretary of defense for international security affairs; and Robert Einhorn, deputy assistant secretary of state for nonproliferation, made clear their desire for legislative relief. During her testimony, Raphel made several references to the ongoing staff discussions on how to best revise the Pressler amendment. Joe Nye made a delicate reference to the need for "fine-tuning" in the legislation to permit improved military-to-military relations.[27] In a somewhat unusual move that underscored the sensitivity of the issue, two other members of Congress addressed the panel in Statements for the Record. Senator Pressler argued against any revision to his amendment, and Representative Lee Hamilton, ranking minority member of the House International Relations Committee, expressed his support for modification or repeal.[28] Scores of interagency briefers also met with staff and shared information papers to help build support for legislative relief.[29]

In Search of a Plan

On April 5, 1995, Prime Minister Bhutto arrived for a weeklong official visit and pressed her "fairness" argument publicly and in private meetings all over the Hill.[30] Her argument struck a sympathetic chord with several members and reinforced the views of Senator Hank Brown, who was already emerging as a strong and vocal proponent of revising the Pressler amendment. On April 11, 1995, President Clinton emerged from a private meeting with Prime Minister Bhutto and declared the situation "unfair." He went on to say, "I don't think it's right for us to keep the money and the equipment. That is not right and I am going to try to find a solution to it. I don't like this."[31] In that moment, with a clear decision from the chief executive now guiding the discussions, the interagency debate shifted from whether to amend Pressler to how.

Ultimately, while rejecting outright repeal as politically untenable, the administration, with Senator Brown's staff, developed a menu of options designed to credibly fulfill the president's commitment in a manner that was legislatively feasible. Some elements of the plan, such as the release of proceeds (approximately $120 million) from the sale of excess parts and components purchased for Pakistan under the sixty-plane contract but never used, and the sale of the F-16s to a third party with the proceeds going back to Pakistan, did not require specific legislative approval.[32] In fact, Senator Pressler had become a proponent of the third-party sale option as a means of resolving the impasse.[33] The administration recognized, however, that the third-party sale of the aircraft would be very difficult since there were few politically acceptable countries that wanted the planes and could afford to pay for them. They needed to do more.

As a result, the proposal included several elements that would require explicit congressional approval. These conditions included release of $368 million of stored military equipment other than the F-16s, waiver of storage costs (as long as there was no budgetary impact), and exemption of all economic and certain types of military assistance (peacekeeping, counternarcotics, antiterrorism) from the Pressler restrictions. Revisions were limited to the Pressler amendment, even though Pakistan continued to face possible sanction from the underlying legislation, namely, the Symington amendment to the Foreign Assistance Act. Since the Symington amendment did not single out Pakistan for sanction, the "fairness" argument simply would not fly, and revisions to that legislation were quickly deemed "too tough."[34]

A "Champion" at Work

On May 23, 1995, after fairly extensive debate, the Senate Foreign Relations Committee voted out a modest version of what would later be known as the Brown amendment. By a vote of 16-2, the committee attached the provision to the Foreign Aid Reduction Act of 1995 (commonly known as the foreign aid authorization bill). Only Senators Paul Sarbanes (D-Md.) and Joseph Biden (D-Del.) opposed the provision, which would lift restrictions on economic assistance and certain types of military assistance. The provision did not include a waiver for the $368 million worth of equipment other than the F-16s that had been trapped in the pipeline when sanctions were imposed. Senator Diane Feinstein (D-Calif.), the ranking minority member on the Near Eastern and South Asian Affairs subcommittee, was supportive of some "nonmilitary" relief for Pakistan but did not support the release of the equipment.[35] As a result, the committee was unlikely to support the entire administration proposal. Even with this scaled-back provision, as the committee was marking up the bill, Senator Pressler made an unexpected appearance to express his reservations about modifying the sanctions and to propose resolving the problem over the F-16 aircraft by selling the planes to a third party.[36]

In the meantime, the administration pressed its solution with the Pakistanis, stressing that this proposal, while not everything Pakistan wanted, was the most that Congress was likely to approve. Throughout July of 1995, the administration discussed the proposal with key members, pushing for a special "one-time" waiver for the equipment other than the F-16s to be added to the modest exemptions already included in the foreign aid authorization bill.[37] The prospects for this legislative vehicle, however, were dim, since the bill included a host of controversial legislation. Besides, Congress had not passed a foreign aid authorization bill since 1985.

Getting the measure to a vote on the Senate floor proved difficult. It took Senator Brown three attempts to pass his amendment in the Senate, which by now included not only the fairly modest revisions that had been approved by the committee but also the release of $368 million worth of equipment (other than the F-16s) that had been in the pipeline when the Bush administration imposed sanctions. The first two tries, on the state authorization bill and the defense authorization bill, were stymied by procedural stalls and threatened filibusters. In both cases,

Senators Glenn and Pressler made prodigious use of personal procedural powers to prevent a Senate vote on the bill. They knew that if Brown's amendment came to a vote, it would probably pass. Neither Senator Pressler nor Senator Glenn would consent to a time agreement, and twice Senator Brown had to withdraw his amendment. In an attempt to defeat the arguments that the equipment would alter the balance of power in South Asia and could be destabilizing (arguments that figured prominently in earlier floor debate), Senator Brown's subcommittee held yet another late-session hearing on the issue.[38]

Finally on September 20, 1995, with the last possible vehicle, the fiscal year 1996 foreign operations bill, on the floor of the Senate, Senator Brown pushed again for his amendment, but he was still unable to secure a time agreement that would allow the vote to proceed under unanimous consent. Without such an agreement the amendment had little chance of getting a vote. Facing yet another filibuster, Senator Brown gave public voice to his frustration, saying:

> We considered this whole question in the drafting of the State Department authorization bill. But when that bill got to the floor, it was filibustered and the President was denied an opportunity to have his proposal. . . . We then offered this package as an amendment to the Defense authorization bill. But the opponents fought that, threatened to filibuster all night, and denied us a vote. . . . What we have seen here is a concerted effort to avoid a vote on this question. . . . an effort by filibustering this amendment to delay the consideration of this vital bill.[39]

To break the impasse, Senator Brown resorted to an unusual and risky procedural technique to see if his amendment could get the sixty votes necessary to break a filibuster. Senator Brown explained his decision on the floor of the Senate: "Mr. President, my suggestion is this: Let us get a vote. If I do not have 60 votes, I am not going to stop this bill or have others filibuster this important piece of legislation just for this amendment. But if we can get 60 votes, then I want this considered, and we will see if we cannot bring closure on this issue."[40] By "moving to table (kill) his own amendment," Senator Brown could "determine if the opposition had the 41 votes needed to sustain a filibuster."[41]

The gamble proved successful when the Senate failed to "table" the amendment by a vote of 37 to 61, indicating that the opposition was four votes short of the forty-one needed to sustain the filibuster. Six hours of debate followed, with Senators Glenn and Pressler leading the opposition. Senator Feinstein struggled to find a "third way" to provide modest legislative relief for Pakistan but prevent the release of the military equipment. Her effort, however, could only garner forty-eight votes, three votes short of the fifty-one votes necessary to modify Brown's provision.[42] Senator Brown's amendment was adopted on a 55-45 vote.[43]

Senator Brown's amendment did spark considerable controversy during the House-Senate conference on the bill, provoking "some of the most vigorous debate in the conference."[44] Although more than forty members signed a letter urging the conferees to reject the Senate language, the measure was approved in late October.[45] Staff and members of the House Appropriations Committee's Subcommittee on Foreign Operations, Export Financing, and Related Programs (commonly called the Foreign Operations Subcommittee) responsible for the bill were fairly sympathetic to the Brown amendment. The provision also enjoyed the support of House Appropriations Committee Chairman Robert Livingston (R-La.).[46] In addition, the administration, particularly Secretary Perry, Chairman of the Joint Chiefs of Staff John Shalikashvili, Deputy National Security Adviser Samuel Berger, Under Secretary of Defense Walter Slocombe, and Assistant Secretary of State Robin Raphel weighed in heavily in support of the amendment.

Even though Senator Brown was not one of the conferees on the bill, he and his principal staffer, Carter Pilcher, played a significant, if not dominant role on this legislation. By agreement between Senator Tom Harkin (D-Iowa) and Senator Brown, Pilcher was allowed into the conference to assist Senator Harkin on this provision.[47] Such a move is highly unusual during an appropriations conference and underscores the central roles of Senator Brown and Carter Pilcher as issue leaders in this case.

In November 1995, Congress approved the fiscal year 1996 foreign operations bill with the original Brown amendment virtually intact. This included a one-time exemption to Pressler, allowing transfer of $368 million worth of equipment to Pakistan that had been embargoed by the Pressler amendment. The amendment also allowed resumption of some limited assistance in support of key areas such as peacekeeping, counterterrorism, and counternarcotics. The twenty-eight F-16s were not included in the deal, but the conference report encouraged the administration to find a new buyer for the planes and to provide the proceeds to Pakistan.

Controversy Erupts

While final approval of the Brown amendment got caught up in the bitter fight over family planning assistance that pitted the House of Representatives against the Senate and the administration, events on the ground in Pakistan were undercutting congressional sympathy for Pakistan. In February 1996, with the ink on the Brown amendment barely dry, further details of Pakistan's acquisition of sensitive nuclear equipment from China appeared in the press. The controversy, sparked by Pakistan's purchase from China of "specialized ring magnets for use in enriching uranium," caused the administration to put implementation of the Brown amendment on hold while members of the administration debated the new information and decided how to respond to the incident.[48]

After an extended interagency debate, on March 19, 1996, the Clinton administration notified Congress that it would release the equipment approved under the Brown amendment despite the ring magnets controversy. Any resumption of new assistance was again on hold since the Symington amendment remained in effect. In an unpublicized meeting, Under Secretary of Defense Walter Slocombe, Deputy National Security Adviser Sandy Berger, and Deputy Secretary of State Strobe Talbott briefed a select group of senators "under tight secrecy rules" to explain the administration's decision and shore up congressional support.[49] The administration's efforts at damage control were fairly successful, and the congressional uproar over the controversy was largely limited to the existing opposition.

On April 17, Deputy Secretary Talbott notified Congress that the administration would deliver the $368 million in equipment that was authorized by the Brown amendment. In addition, the United States would return $120 million in cash that had been realized from the sale to third countries of excess F-16 components purchased for Pakistan but that had never been used.[50] Talbott explained that because of concerns about "the transfer of nuclear equipment from China to Pakistan," the administration would not release any of the economic assistance funds authorized by the Brown amendment.[51]

What to Do about the F-16s?

Still eager to clear the books with Pakistan and fulfill the president's commitment, the administration spent much of spring 1996 on a plan to sell Pakistan's F-16s to a third party and to return the proceeds to Pakistan. As Defense Department officials pointed out, such a deal was much harder than it would appear. The significant depreciation of the planes while they had been sitting in storage almost guaranteed that the return to Pakistan would be less than fifty cents on the dollar.[52] Moreover, they needed a cash buyer to make the plan work, but since most of the qualified buyers were not interested in acquiring old aircraft, only a tremendous discount would make them attractive. Finally, as one Pentagon official explained, "These planes were directly competing with hundreds of excess aircraft from the Air Force inventory that could generate revenue for the Air Force."[53] As a result, the U.S. Air Force had little incentive to push the sale of these particular planes.

After extensive negotiations, Indonesia emerged as the most likely (and probably only) buyer for the planes, and a draft agreement was completed in June 1996.[54] Before the congressional notifications could be made, however, Indonesia cracked down on political activists in the country, prompting an outcry in Congress. Staff from the House International Relations Committee and the Senate Foreign Relations Committee quickly warned the State Department not to forward the necessary notifications or they would be placed on hold. As is the tradition in almost all arms transfer cases, the State Department was expected to respect the hold or risk retribution in this or other areas. Fearing a backlash, the department did not send the notifications, the session ended, and, in the end, the Indonesians withdrew their support for the plan.[55]

Passage of the Brown amendment was a legislative success, but its policy impact has been far less impressive than its proponents hoped and expected. Pakistani actions on proliferation greatly complicated efforts to seek a waiver of the Symington sanctions. These sanctions prohibited implementation of the modest assistance activities and military education and training that the Brown amendment envisioned. In the fiscal year 1998 foreign operations appropriations bill, Senator Harkin led an effort to permit a partial waiver of the Symington sanctions. The provision was designed to exempt international military education and training from the Symington amendment and enjoyed strong support from the Department of Defense and the joint staff. At the last minute, however, Representative Pelosi successfully eliminated the provision from the fiscal year 1998 foreign operations conference report. [56]

Finally, in the fall of 1998, Congress passed an amendment sponsored by Representative Sam Brownback (R-Kans.) that provided limited waiver authority for the Glenn and Symington amendments following India's and Pakistan's nuclear tests in the spring of 1998. The F-16 issue remained a sore point in U.S.-Pakistani relations until December 1998, when Pakistan agreed to a U.S. proposal to settle the matter out of court for approximately $325 million in cash. At last report, New Zealand may be interested in leasing the aircraft.

Lessons

The Brown amendment is a graphic example of the power of issue leaders and the importance of a strong champion to support foreign policy legislation. From 1990 to 1995, nonproliferationists such as Senator Glenn and Senator Pressler dominated the Pakistan issue in Congress. Throughout the 1980s, anticommunist, promujahideen members of Congress provided a powerful counterweight to the nonproliferation argument. With the demise of the Soviet Union and the end of the cold war, this counterweight was gone. As a result, earlier executive branch attempts to resolve the dispute by rewriting the Foreign Assistance Act or releasing the F-16s in exchange for certain nonproliferation-related agreements were easily rebuffed. With such strong issue leaders opposing any revision to the Pressler amendment, legislative relief seemed hopeless.

In 1995, when Senator Brown emerged as a strong advocate of sanctions relief for Pakistan, the dynamics shifted dramatically. One could argue that Senator Brown's role as champion for revising the Pressler amendment was the single most important factor in getting the legislation passed. Senator Brown's highly focused, determined, and sometimes uncompromising personality was well known in the Senate. One staffer who was close to the process credits the success of the initiative almost exclusively to these "personality factors," saying that "once the Senator took hold of any issue he was reluctant to let go."[57] That was certainly the case. Senator Brown, along with his staffer Carter Pilcher, pursued the issue doggedly, with a devotion that had previously been limited to the opposition—Senator Glenn and his staffer Randy Rydell. Another staffer who observed the process explains, "Carter Pilcher was relent-less. He was hell-bent on this issue and would not be deterred."[58] Sena-tor Brown's position as chairman of the Subcommittee on Near Eastern and South Asian Affairs of the Senate Foreign Relations Committee was helpful, especially because it gave him considerable control over the hearings schedule, but it was not essential to his role as an issue leader. Personality, more than position, was the deciding factor.

Senator Brown's opposition made impressive use of the Senate's indi-vidual powers (in the form of filibusters and holds), successfully pre-venting a vote on two occasions and nearly preventing the third. As a result, Senator Brown had to use an unusual and risky maneuver (a motion to table his own amendment) to break the filibuster and force a vote by demonstrating that he had the votes to invoke cloture. Senator Brown's maneuvers may have been unusual, but they were not impromptu. As one staffer who observed the vote explains, "You have to give them credit, they were very well prepared. They had been whip-ping that vote for months."[59]

Disentangling the motivations of the key members involved is diffi-cult. But it is clear that knee-jerk assumptions about ethnic politics, elec-toral motivations, and partisan allegiances have little merit. Neither Pressler nor Brown had significant numbers of Indian or Pakistani con-stituents to motivate their interest in the subcontinent. Senator Brown became a champion of Pakistan and the effort to revise legislative restrictions on U.S. assistance to Pakistan during his final term in office. Since he had announced his retirement, his electoral prospects could hardly have been pertinent. Even though Senator Pressler actively sought to use his position on the Brown amendment to generate cam-paign funds from the Indian-American community, the hero status that both men assumed in the countries whose positions they advocated was of little electoral benefit.[60] Senator Pressler lost his seat in the next elec-tion, and Senator Brown retired as planned at the end of his term.

Partisan affiliations also proved to be poor predictors of support or opposition. The administration's most robust opposition came from fel-low Democrats, particularly Senator Feinstein and Senator Glenn, who worked with Senator Pressler. The administration's ally and champion was a Republican who proved willing to take on the "sacred cow" of a fellow Republican. Some of Senator Brown's strongest support in the Senate came from a liberal Democrat, Senator Tom Harkin of Iowa, who went so far as to allow Carter Pilcher (a Republican staffer) to assist his efforts on behalf of the issue during the conference. In this competition among issue leaders, the strongly expressed preferences of the executive branch made a clear difference, especially for Senate fence-sitters and House conferees, but they would have been for naught if the measure had a less ardent champion. Issue loyalties were clearly the dominant factor.

Senator Brown's emergence as a champion shifted the center of gravity away from Senator Glenn and Senator Pressler and gave administration regionalists and pro-Pakistani interest groups outside of government a "place to go." Once the Pakistani government and its U.S. lobbyists (not to mention the executive branch) found an ally in Senator Brown, they actively cultivated a close working relationship by providing information, data, and early warning. Senator Brown returned the favor by carefully vetting his proposals and strategies with both the executive branch and the Pakistani embassy.[61]

The effort to secure passage of the Brown amendment provides a classic case of "issue cluster" competition. Since the issue never rose to the level of an institutional or political "loyalty test," the conflict remained primarily within the policy sphere where cross-party and cross-institutional linkages thrive. In this battle, congressional nonproliferation leaders such as Senator Pressler, Senator Glenn and his staffer Randy Rydell, various arms control organizations, the pro-India lobbyists, and some disgruntled nonproliferation advocates in the executive branch squared off against Senator Brown, Carter Pilcher, the majority of the administration, and the pro-Pakistan lobbyists. Both sides of the controversy relied extensively on the vast array of interest groups, nongovernmental organizations, and even paid lobbyists for information, research, and early warning. Moreover, as the issue came to a head in a Senate vote, these organizations and lobbyists were highly effective in reaching out to other members. Close collaboration of issue groups, particularly in their information-gathering and early warning capacity, was evident throughout the process but most prominently during the Senate's floor debate.

The recent history of the Pressler and Brown amendments provides useful examples—positive and negative—of how Congress and the executive cooperate to make foreign policy. The highly contentious interagency process involving the rewrite of the Foreign Assistance Act and the decision to remove the Pressler language from the administration's formal legislative submission should have provided a better indicator of congressional reaction. Administration proponents of the rewrite of the Foreign Assistance Act no sooner quelled the nonproliferationist voices (particularly the Arms Control and Disarmament Agency) within the administration than they faced the issue all over again upon sending the bill to Congress. Nonproliferationists may have lost the interagency battle, but they won the "war" when the administration capitulated and reversed its position on the Pressler amendment in the face of congressional hostility.

Two years later, an informal, collaborative process that lined up a congressional champion to take on the Pressler amendment was much more successful. Informal conversations between Senator Brown and the secretary of defense were a catalyst for a significant effort to revise legislative restrictions on U.S assistance to Pakistan. The senator's staff worked closely and informally with officials in the State Department and the Defense Department on the details of the legislation as it wound its way through the legislative process. Extensive consultations and briefings helped to broaden the base of congressional support.

To its credit, the administration used the informal system effectively. Proponents of legislative relief for Pakistan also employed a deliberate strategy to keep the legislation as narrow and technical as possible and to build support through a congressional champion rather than an "administration initiative." Representatives from the administration and Senator Brown's staff worked collaboratively and informally on the legislation during the legislative process. Finally, when the ring magnets controversy threatened to derail the entire process, the executive branch used high-level consultations with congressional leaders to sustain support for the decision to proceed with releasing the equipment. With the leadership on board and the legislation in hand, the administration could fend off the vocal criticisms of opponents and mitigate their ability to exercise informal power to affect the policy.

SIX　　　　　*The Chemical Weapons*
　　　　　　　Convention

ON JANUARY 13, 1993, as one of his final acts as president, George Bush signed the Chemical Weapons Convention (CWC), a sweeping international treaty prohibiting the development, production, acquisition, stockpiling, retention, transfer, and use of chemical weapons.[1] After President Clinton assumed office, the new National Security Council staff wanted to ratify the treaty quickly in hopes of securing an early victory for the new president's nonproliferation policy. The treaty was supposed to be a sure winner. It had a stack of bipartisan credentials and an unassailable political message. Who could be against getting rid of chemical weapons? In June 1989, seventy-four senators (well over the two-thirds majority needed to support ratification) had written to President Bush urging him to complete an international chemical weapons ban.[2]

Ultimately, the process was anything but easy. The effort to secure Senate consent to the Chemical Weapons Convention became one of the most contentious and protracted legislative battles of the Clinton presidency.[3] The effort to ratify the convention has all the classic characteristics of a wave—high-profile institutional conflict, formal processes and requirements, extensive media attention, and high-stakes political gamesmanship. Yet, the CWC cannot be understood solely in these terms. During the four-year ratification process, the CWC spent far more time in the foreign policy trenches than it did in the political stratosphere. Media attention and public interest were intense but intermittent. While the conflict eventually became an institutional contest, powerful individual issue leaders, using all the informal and procedural powers at their disposal, drove the process. Moreover, despite the political and institutional overtones of the CWC debate, cross-institutional linkages and issue clusters played a major role throughout the period.

Interagency Fumbling

President Clinton's National Security Council staff wanted to submit the Chemical Weapons Convention to the Senate as soon as possible after the inauguration, but the treaty bogged down for several months as various interagency players wrangled over the details of the article-by-article analysis of the treaty and the implementing legislation.[4] The situation was exacerbated by general disarray in the administration's foreign policy apparatus, as new appointees moved slowly through the confirmation process. Numerous foreign policy crises in Somalia, Bosnia, and elsewhere absorbed most senior-level attention. In addition, some of the president's advisers were nervous that the treaty could fall victim to an "odd-couple alliance" between Senate conservatives who might oppose the treaty and a number of Senate Democrats who had reservations about the domestic chemical demilitarization. Some White House officials also were arguing that the administration could not push hard on the Chemical Weapons Convention until the Senate ratified the strategic arms reduction talks (START II), or it would risk losing both treaties. As it happens, the Senate did not ratify START II until January 1996.[5]

In the rush to complete the treaty, the Bush administration had deferred some controversial interagency issues, insisting that they could be handled in the materials that accompanied the treaty for ratification. Foremost among them was a long-standing dispute over the use of riot control agents (RCAs). Through much of 1993, mid-level National Security Council officials engaged in a highly acrimonious interagency battle to finalize work on the treaty and get it to Congress. This effort included an attempt to clarify the range of permitted uses of riot control agents. While the National Security Council, Department of Defense, and Department of State quickly determined that the treaty would permit the use of these agents against rioting prisoners of war, Defense Department and military officials felt strongly that RCAs provided essential protection for U.S. soldiers, particularly downed pilots, from civilian mobs. They also felt strongly that RCAs were essential when enemy combatants used civilians as "screens." On these two issues inter-agency consensus proved elusive.[6]

The issue was so contentious that the treaty was submitted to the Senate on November 23, 1993, just days before the end of the session, with the RCA issue still outstanding.[7] The issue was not resolved until June 1994 when Chairman of the Joint Chiefs of Staff John Shalikashvili sided with the National Security Council and agreed to a narrower interpretation, prompting what one official involved in the dispute called "a near mutiny among the Joint Chiefs."[8] The council's victory on the RCA issue would eventually prove empty as the seeds of opposition to the treaty were now sown, and significant military and veteran support for the treaty would not be forthcoming until the RCA issue was renegotiated in 1997.

On March 22, 1994, the Senate Foreign Relations Committee held its first hearing on the Chemical Weapons Convention. While a number of members showed up to hear Secretary of State Warren Christopher testify in support of the treaty and urge ratification by July 17, the entire session lasted only half an hour. Senator Claiborne Pell (D-R.I.), chairman of the committee, was the only member present at the next hearing on April 13, 1994, with Stephen J. Ledogar, chief U.S. negotiator for the treaty. The apparent disinterest prompted David Morrison of the *National Journal* to comment, "The almost eerily stealthy fashion in which the 'chemical convention' . . . is wending its way through" the Senate is "little short of startling."[9]

Fax Attacks

By late 1994, Frank Gaffney and his small but prolific Center for Security Policy were beginning to gear up in opposition to the CWC, attacking the treaty as unverifiable, inadequate, and expensive. Many treaty devotees discounted Gaffney's effort as inconsequential, ignoring that Gaffney had a small but loyal following on Capitol Hill and that he had been successful in other "fax wars" such as his effort to prevent Morton Halperin from becoming an assistant secretary of defense in 1993. Unable to see the threat to the treaty lurking just over the horizon, the ratification effort drifted. Within the administration, the president's top national security team was preoccupied with events in Haiti, Cuba, Bosnia, and Somalia. Moreover, as one official explains, "There was no single [Commander-in-

Chief] Ratification" empowered to oversee the effort at a lower level.[10] The treaty's Senate champion, Chairman Pell, showed limited enthusiasm, and the Senate's Democratic leadership was preoccupied with the increasingly ominous prospects for the 1994 elections.

Meanwhile, the RCA controversy with the Pentagon continued, and the White House's reluctance to speak frankly about any of the treaty's drawbacks undermined executive branch unity on the treaty. Concerns among the military services about the limits on RCAs spilled over to Congress, particularly to Senator Sam Nunn (D-Ga.) and the Senate Armed Services Committee, where reservations about the treaty began to surface. The National Security Council's handling of the RCA issue reinforced an impression among congressional Democrats and Republicans (particularly those serving on the armed services committees), that the Clinton administration was "rolling" the military on issues such as gays in the military and Defense Department support for peacekeeping and other activities traditionally funded by the State Department. This controversy, along with other minor concerns about the treaty, created apprehension that ratification might not be easy and greatly contributed to the decision by Senator Pell and the Senate Foreign Relations Committee to delay the vote until the next session. According to one Senate staffer, "The administration's mishandling of the RCA issue is the primary reason that the CWC did not get ratified while the Democrats controlled the Senate."[11] The controversy caused delay, which proved particularly damaging in the second half of an election year when competition for the legislative calendar is fierce. Meanwhile, a number of the president's senior advisers felt that START II should be the priority treaty. As a result, another year passed without action on the CWC.

The Battle with Senator Jesse Helms

The November 1994 elections brought the Senate under Republican control and the Senate Foreign Relations Committee under the leadership of North Carolina Senator Jesse Helms. Relations between the State Department and Senator Helms had always been prickly. During Helms's tenure as the ranking minority member of the Senate Foreign Relations Committee, however, the executive branch had been able to ignore many of his contrarian views on foreign policy, often looking to the more prominent "internationalist" Republican on the panel, Senator

Richard Lugar (R-Ind.). With Senator Helms as chairman, that would now prove impossible.

In January 1995, Congress was barely back in session before the battle lines were drawn over the new chairman's determined effort to overhaul the government's foreign policy apparatus by reorganizing the State Department and its associated agencies—the Arms Control and Disarmament Agency (ACDA), the U.S. Agency for International Development (USAID), and the U.S. Information Agency (USIA). Senator Helms argued that the idea originally came from the administration, which had examined and rejected the idea of agency consolidation. While true, the administration bitterly opposed a congressionally mandated reorganization, which it regarded as excessive. With Senator Helms determined to pass legislation on reorganization that year and the administration equally determined to reject any legislatively mandated reorganization, the situation deteriorated into a bitter, angry stalemate.[12]

While Chairman Pell had been fairly timid in his use of the prerogatives and procedures of the chairmanship and the Senate, Senator Helms showed no similar restraint. The administration, for its part, was slow to accept the senator's intention to make his mark on foreign policy and reclaim a seat for the Senate Foreign Relations Committee and its chairman at the policymaking table. This would include making far more aggressive use of the committee's responsibilities for nominations and treaties as a means of leverage. As one staffer explained, "Senator Helms had an agenda and he was not afraid to use all of the levers at his disposal to advance that agenda."[13] The administration seemed surprised that Republican leadership did not do more to isolate and temper Chairman Helms, failing to understand how the reorganization proposal, as well as other issues (international family planning, peacekeeping, the United Nations) genuinely resonated with much of the Republican leadership. Moreover, the institutional traditions and prerogatives of the Senate made it extremely difficult to curtail the chairman's use of his prerogatives.

Unable to muster the sixty votes necessary to invoke cloture and limit debate, Senator Helms fumed while Senate Democrats successfully filibustered his reorganization bill all summer, preventing it from coming to a vote in the Senate. Helms then retaliated by putting all ambassadorial nominations and all treaties (including START II and the Chemical Weapons Convention) on hold.[14] Long and tortured negotiations yielded no results, and the stalemate continued through the fall. With Senate action on foreign policy at a standstill for more than five months, Democrats began to ratchet up the stakes with Senator Jeff Bingaman (D-N.M.) filibustering a constitutional amendment on flag desecration.[15]

A Surprise Maneuver

Finally in mid-September, with the high-priority fiscal year 1996 foreign operations appropriations bill also under a filibuster threat, Senator John Kerry (D-Mass.) and Chairman Helms negotiated a unanimous consent agreement that allowed the foreign operations bill to go forward, freed up some of the ambassadorial nominations, and guaranteed a Senate vote on a version of the reorganization legislation.[16] On December 14, after more than ten weeks of tortured negotiations between Senator Kerry, Chairman Helms, and the administration, the Senate voted out a modified version of Senator Helms's State Department reorganization bill. In exchange, the chairman agreed to lift the embargo on treaties and nominations, including a guarantee that the CWC would be reported out of committee by April 30, 1996.[17]

Initially, Senator Helms's personal opposition to the CWC, while evident, appeared to be secondary to his desire to advance his reorganization effort. The agreement to trade CWC for the reorganization legislation, however, prompted a bitter fight among the staff of the Senate Foreign Relations Committee and resulted in a decision to "de-link" the two issues.[18] By the time Senator Helms turned his full attention to the treaty in March, his opposition had solidified. By then, at the urging of the Center for Security Policy, a small but influential and devoted band of opponents, including Senators Jon Kyl (R-Ariz.) and Strom Thurmond (R-S.C.), had begun to emerge.

To most observers, however, the treaty still looked like a fairly "easy sell" in early 1996.[19] The reasons were clear. First, the treaty had a strong bipartisan pedigree. It was negotiated by Presidents Ronald Reagan and George Bush, signed by President Bush, and submitted and strongly supported by President Clinton. In addition, since existing law required the elimination of almost all chemical weapons in the United States by 2004, the treaty had little direct impact (outside of the RCA issue) on the U.S. military. Finally, the treaty had strong support from major chemical companies whose factories would be subject to inspection and verification requirements. These companies had been closely consulted during the treaty's negotiation process, and they had a lot to lose if the United States was cut out of the implementation process. If the United States failed to ratify the CWC before the treaty entered into force, then the United States could lose its ability to shape the administration and implementation of the treaty, and U.S. chemical companies could face major disadvantages vis-à-vis their international competitors.

In March, the administration began a concerted push for ratification, and committee action on the treaty began in earnest. In a March 28 joint appearance, Secretary of Defense William Perry and Secretary of State Warren Christopher urged the Senate to ratify the treaty.[20] On April 25, 1996, the Senate Foreign Relations Committee met to consider the treaty. The chairman's resolution of ratification included numerous revisions and qualification that would effectively "gut" the treaty. Led by Senator Lugar, the panel unexpectedly rejected the chairman's "mark" (draft legislation) by a vote of 13 to 5. Senator Lugar then offered a substitute resolution, which was supported by the administration. The committee passed Senator Lugar's resolution by a vote of 12 to 6. Senators Chuck Hagel (R-Nebr.), Gordon Smith (R-Ore.), Craig Thomas (R-Wyo.), and Bill Frist (R-Tenn.) joined Senator Lugar and all of the committee Democrats in opposing the chairman's mark.[21]

Senator Helms had the power of the chairmanship and the prerogatives of the Senate at his disposal, but he did not have the votes in committee to drive the issue where he wanted it to go. Senator Lugar's maneuver was a great victory for treaty proponents, but opponents had reason to crow as well. Republicans were now deeply divided over the treaty. As one Senate staffer explains, "By April, 1996 the critical distinction between the Reagan and Bush Republicans on the CWC had emerged."[22] Bolstered by Senator Lugar's success in the Senate Foreign Relations Committee, the administration chose to work closely with him and his staff. CWC supporters had broken through a critical barrier by moving the resolution out of committee, but the two-thirds majority needed to pass the resolution of ratification was already in jeopardy. The terms of the December unanimous consent agreement had been met, and the battle now moved to the Senate leadership as Senator Robert Dole (R-Kans.), preoccupied with his presidential election bid and impending resignation from the Senate, proved reluctant to find time on the Senate calendar for the treaty.

The CWC Goes Political

By June 1996, almost all defense and foreign policy legislation was locked in a tangle of filibusters and counterfilibusters as treaty supporters and proponents used every available vehicle as a hostage to push their case. Finally, Thomas Daschle (D-S.D.), Senate minority leader, threatened to filibuster the fiscal year 1997 defense authorization bill and prevent any kind of Senate vote on national missile defense (NMD), which was an election year priority for Senator Trent Lott (R-Miss.), the newly elected Senate majority leader. The deadlock had to be broken.

On June 28, 1996, the two senators agreed to a unanimous consent agreement on national missile defenses and the Chemical Weapons Convention. Under the agreement, the highly contentious missile defense provisions of the defense authorization bill (which were considered "veto-bait" by the administration) were dropped with the assurance that Democrats would not filibuster a stand-alone National Missile Defense Act that would come to the floor separately. The unanimous consent agreement also provided that the CWC would come to a vote in the Senate before September 14.[23] The high-stakes procedural wrangling that produced the agreement did little to encourage comity and negotiation on the treaty. Treaty supporters focused so exclusively on getting the treaty to the floor that they failed to recognize they were losing the votes to secure ratification.

Throughout this period, the administration worked closely, almost exclusively, with Senator Lugar (R-Ind.) as the treaty's champion. It was here that the administration made a critical miscalculation. As one administration official explains, "We were working hard with Senator Lugar and trusted that all Republican votes counted equally. We were wrong. Senator Lugar just was not part of the 'in crowd' with Senator Lott."[24]

By the summer of 1996, bipartisanship on the Chemical Weapons Convention was disintegrating, and many Republicans were reluctant to give a big legislative win to the president so soon before the election. Meanwhile the gulf was widening among Republicans over the treaty. Former secretary of defense Richard Cheney took many people by surprise, including a number of Defense Department officials who worked for him under the Bush administration, when he came out against the treaty he had helped to negotiate. Explained one such official, "These were the same people who when we took the same concerns to them in

1992 said 'Back off, this is the President's treaty.' Now four years later they were rejecting the very treaty they had approved."[25]

Recognizing that conditions for the treaty were deteriorating, officials in the National Security Council tried to raise the rhetorical stakes by building up the role the CWC might play in preventing chemical and biological terrorism. Over the objections of several midlevel officials who felt the substantive links to domestic terrorism were tenuous, Secretary of Defense Perry and Attorney General Janet Reno coauthored an op-ed that implied that the convention could help prevent events like the 1995 use of sarin (a deadly nerve agent) in a terrorist attack in the Tokyo subway.[26] Widely perceived as an attempt to embarrass "fence-sitting" Republicans, this gamble further contributed to the politicization of the issue and prompted angry reactions from several Republican senators working to support the treaty. As one treaty opponent explained, "We knew about the op-ed in advance and countered the argument easily. There is no question that it helped our case and worked against the administration."[27]

Shortly thereafter, the National Federation of Independent Business expressed opposition to the treaty, warning that its reporting requirements could unreasonably burden many smaller businesses. The organization provided the necessary probusiness counterweight to the chemical manufacturers, who supported the treaty, to knock a few more senators off the block.[28]

Finally on September 11, Republican presidential candidate Dole unexpectedly came out against the Chemical Weapons Convention, making it increasingly unlikely that many fence-sitting Republicans would want to support the treaty. This turned out to be the proverbial final nail in the coffin. Desperate to get the treaty passed, the Clinton administration took it down to the wire but asked that the treaty be withdrawn on September 12, two days before the scheduled vote, when vote counts indicated that the treaty would be defeated.[29] The administration had no choice since a negative vote in the Senate probably would have sunk the treaty for good.

At least one official acknowledged that Senator Lott did the administration a favor by preventing a vote the administration certainly would have lost.[30] But the administration paid a heavy price for pulling back at the last minute. Senator Lott could now hold the administration (and congressional Democrats) to their agreement on missile defenses, while offering no terms or timetable for reconsidering the treaty. The administration had no choice but to start from scratch and pick up the pieces after the election. Furthermore, with the start of a new Congress, the CWC was sent back to the Senate Foreign Relations Committee and back into the arms of its archrival, Senator Jesse Helms. Senator Lugar's previous efforts to get the treaty out of committee were now for naught, and treaty supporters would have to start over.

Starting Over with the Clock Ticking

On October 31, 1996, Hungary became the sixty-fifth country to ratify the CWC, initiating a six-month countdown until the treaty would enter into force. Unless the United States ratified the treaty before April 29, 1997, it would be shut out of the administration of the treaty, lose access to intelligence resulting from the declaration and inspection process, and lose its vote within the treaty's governing body.[31] The administration and the Senate now had a firm deadline to focus debate. With the clock ticking, the administration and its new foreign policy leadership finally began to develop a concerted game plan to get the treaty passed.

This new approach contained five critical elements. First, the administration shifted to a negotiation-based rather than a confrontation-based strategy with Congress. Central to this approach was the decision by the new national security adviser, Samuel Berger, to ask Robert Bell, special assistant to the president and senior director for defense programs and arms control, to assume lead responsibility for negotiating the treaty with the Senate. With many years of experience in the Senate, Bell had the patience and experience for the hours of tedious negotiation the treaty would require.

Second, the administration developed and pursued an aggressive public and special interest strategy to shore up the national consensus in support of the treaty. Borrowing a page from the playbook on the North American Free Trade Agreement, the White House set up the White House Working Group on the Chemical Weapons Convention to coordinate efforts with nongovernmental organizations and interest groups and to respond quickly to claims and accusations by treaty opponents. The working group's "blast faxes" countered and helped to diffuse Frank Gaffney's previously unanswered fax attacks. Coupled with the nineteen "Dear colleague" letters put out by Senator Lugar challenging the arguments put forward by treaty opponents, treaty supporters began to retake the momentum.[32]

Third, new Secretary of State Madeleine Albright made clear her intention to develop a more constructive working relationship with Senator Helms and his committee. Starting with her confirmation hearing, Albright made it clear that she would keep an open mind on the reorganization issue and would not be bound by former secretary Christopher's position. Fourth, the administration toned down the rhetoric it used to describe the treaty. The "warts and all" approach that emphasized the simple concept we are "better with it than without it" was convincingly put forward by new Secretary of Defense William Cohen. This more realistic description drew a wider net of support than the more ambitious claims that the treaty was a cure-all for a variety of nonproliferation and terrorism ills. Finally, the president and his national security team gave the treaty the kind of high-level, focused attention that treaty proponents had spent the last three years demanding. A constant barrage of speeches, television appearances, op-eds, and other statements from the president on down made clear that this time they were serious.

Treaty opponents, however, were certainly not giving up. As one staffer on the Senate Foreign Relations Committee explains, "In round one [1996] we were still on defense, in round two we went on the offensive."[33] Senator Helms actively used his prerogatives as the committee chair to control the committee calendar and prevent committee consideration of the resolution of ratification. With a majority of the Senate Foreign Relations Committee members opposing the chairman on the treaty, however, the issue was deadlocked within the committee. Senator Helms could stall and delay the treaty, but he could not muster the votes to pass an alternative resolution. As a result, Senator Helms worked with the majority leader to create an alternative and more favorable forum to consider the treaty. Senator Lott established a Chemical Weapons Convention task force that had primary responsibility for identifying areas of disagreement and negotiating the resolution of ratification. The task force was staffed primarily with treaty opponents and deliberately excluded the treaty's Republican champion, Senator Richard Lugar.

The Two-Track Approach

By January 1997 the ratification effort had split into two clearly delineated tracks. On the inside track, Robert Bell led detailed and painstaking negotiations, with the CWC task force gradually consolidating areas of disagreement into "understandings" that could be accepted by the administration and "killer amendments" that would be voted on by the Senate during the ratification debate. By isolating the most serious changes to the treaty in these amendments, the treaty proponents would only have to muster fifty-one votes to defeat them. According to a senior official involved in the process, "The administration caught the task force by surprise and put some real concessions on the table early. That seemed to improve the climate and convince the task force that we were serious."[34] Publicly, Helms was still playing hardball and holding out to kill the treaty altogether, but secretly he instructed his staff to go ahead and negotiate and get as much as they could in the resolution of ratification.[35]

Senator Lugar, while formally excluded from the negotiations, was personally briefed by Bell after every meeting.[36] Though agreeing on little else, both treaty supporters and opponents on the Hill were united in their assessment that the appointment of a single, centralized administration authority to oversee the effort generally and the personal skills and Senate experience of Bell specifically were significant in deciding the fate of the treaty. Said one staffer on the opposing side, "Once we were drawn to the negotiating table with Bob Bell, we knew what the final outcome would be; it was just a matter of getting the best deal we could."[37] At the same time, the State Department, the Defense Department, and the rest of the interagency players were largely cut out of the National Security Council's direct negotiations with Congress, although they did "buttress the effort" with briefings and discussions with congressional staffers.[38]

The battle for public opinion was a much broader effort. According to one agency official involved in the process, most of the State Department's and the Defense Department's efforts on behalf of the treaty were devoted to outreach. For example, much of the Department of Defense's effort was concentrated on shoring up support with the veterans and military organizations and reassuring them that the RCA issue had now been resolved favorably and would not be a threat to American troops.[39] Working levels, however, did carry on many informal staff discussions.[40]

Meanwhile, the many nongovernmental organizations with a stake in the treaty organized into several ad hoc coalitions designed solely to secure ratification of the CWC. The Poison Gas Task Force, based at the

Henry L. Stimson Center, was created to coordinate public education on the CWC. A second coalition, the Monday Lobby, allowed those organizations not constrained by tax laws on nonprofits to coordinate their lobbying activities. In addition, the National Security News Service "sent over eight-hundred information packets on the CWC to editorial writers around the country. . . . This editorial campaign helped garner 171 editorials in 102 newspapers supporting the CWC."[41]

Both sides fought tooth and nail for high-profile endorsements, especially among prominent Republicans and retired military officers. Treaty opponents produced some dramatic testimony on April 8, 1997, when three former defense secretaries, James Schlesinger, Caspar W. Weinberger, and Donald Rumsfeld, testified against the CWC. The White House also scored a number of endorsement successes, such as the April 4 presidential news conference with former secretary of state James Baker.[42] The advocacy group, Business Executives for National Security, proved to be a formidable player by delivering important high-profile endorsements, such as those from Generals Norman Schwartzkopf and Colin Powell, and by shoring up opposition to the notion that the treaty was somehow "bad for business."[43]

On April 10, 1997, Senator Lott announced the basic terms of a deal for bringing the treaty to the floor for debate. First, during the week of April 14, the Senate would consider a bill sponsored by Senator Jon Kyl (R-Ariz.) that would enact some CWC provisions as U.S. law. This was a concession by treaty supporters because of their concern that the legislation would provide political cover to some members wanting to vote against the treaty. Second, the Senate would take up the resolution of ratification during the week of April 21 with fifteen hours of general debate, including a closed session for classified information. The resolution of ratification would include twenty-eight already-negotiated "understandings." The Senate would debate and vote on five "fatal" understandings as amendments. Finally, the administration agreed to submit modifications to two other arms control treaties, the Conventional Forces in Europe flank agreement and the Antiballistic Missile Treaty Demarcation agreement, to the Senate as treaty amendments—an issue that had been a long-standing source of disagreement between the administration and Senator Lott.[44]

Throughout this period, Senator Helms, while participating in the negotiations, was still trying to prevent the treaty from ever coming to a vote. It was more than a week before Helms lifted his hold and assented to the unanimous consent agreement necessary to allow debate to proceed. "Coincidentally," Senator Helms dropped his opposition to the April 24 vote on April 17, the same day he reached agreement with the White House and State Department on the reorganization legislation.[45] Both sides insisted that there was no quid pro quo, and it may be true. First, the senator's staff was as reluctant as the administration to "trade" CWC for anything. Second, Senator Lott was under enormous pressure to allow the debate and give the treaty its vote. Further delay was politically unsustainable. Notably, the majority leader discharged the treaty from the Senate Foreign Relations Committee as part of the unanimous consent agreement governing the debate. The committee did not act on the treaty, in part because Senator Helms could not be sure that he could sustain his position.[46] Nevertheless, the agreement on the reorganization clearly improved the atmosphere for the treaty's passage.

No endorsement was sought more aggressively than that of former senator Dole, whose opposition to the treaty while he was the Republican presidential candidate had torpedoed the earlier vote. Upon hearing that Dole might be amenable to changing his position, Bell provided the former senator with an extensive briefing on the state of the negotiations. On April 23, Dole appeared with President Clinton to announce his support for the treaty, stating that his earlier concerns had been addressed and improved by the agreed understandings.[47] Treaty opponents were devastated.

While playing a prominent role in negotiations with the White House, Senator Lott held his cards very close. One principal staffer in the opposition effort said, "We knew that Lott would not be with us way back in November [1996], we just were not getting the right signals."[48] Supporters insisted, however, that they did not know what Senator Lott would do right up to the day of the vote. Moreover, according to protreaty staff, "The way that Lott gave control of the task force and floor debate to treaty opponents clearly stacked the deck against the treaty."[49] Views within the executive branch about Senator Lott's role are similarly divergent. Since it was assumed by both sides that the Senate majority leader would swing six to eight votes with him, the ambiguity of his position made it impossible to get an accurate vote count in the lead-up to the debate and kept both sides guessing. Thus it is not surprising that on April 18, 1997, only six days before the vote, Daschle, the Senate minority leader, was quoted as saying, "My assessment is that there is a 50-50 chance we can pass the treaty next week—no better than that. . . . Clearly this is not in the bag yet. We've got a long way to go, and I'm very concerned about it."[50]

In the final days leading up to the debate, the president lobbied at least twenty-five senators personally. Finally, on the day of the vote, the administration secured Senator Lott's support for the treaty by sending a letter from President Clinton citing additional circumstances under which he would withdraw from the treaty. On April 24, 1997, the U.S. Senate voted 74 to 26 to ratify the Chemical Weapons Convention.[51]

The implementing legislation passed the Senate shortly thereafter on May 23, 1997.[52] It passed the House on November 12, 1997, but only with a controversial rider attached involving proliferation sanctions toward Russia and Iran. The Senate passed a similar version on May 22, 1998, by an overwhelming margin, and the House again passed the legislation on June 9, 1998, by a vote of 392 to 22. Finally in the fall of 1998, a year and a half after the treaty was ratified, Congress passed the implementing legislation as part of the fiscal year 1999 omnibus appropriations bill.

Implications

Ratification of the Chemical Weapons Convention was certainly a full-scale "wave"—a genuine institutional challenge that transcended individual power. Unlike most foreign policy issues, this contentious ratification process triggered considerable media coverage, particularly as crucial votes approached in September 1996 and April 1997. The issue played out publicly and formally, culminating in a formal vote of ratification. At the end of the day the institution spoke and supported the president. As the tortured machinations and agonizing process described make clear, however, the Chemical Weapons Convention was hardly a simple "victory" for the president. Formal hearings and vote counts simply do not tell the story.

To understand what happened to the Chemical Weapons Convention, we must place this institutional clash in the context of the informal universe. Despite the treaty's formal and public characteristics, a remarkably small number of staff and members drove the agenda for an issue that gripped both branches of government at the highest levels. It is impossible to separate the events surrounding the CWC from the individual personalities from both branches who were involved. Issue leaders were central to the debate and were the driving force behind the controversy. Senators Jesse Helms, Jon Kyl, and Richard Lugar and a few key staffers dominated the entire debate largely through the use of individual power and their keen interest in and knowledge about the issues, rather than through their institutional roles.

Procedural techniques and individual powers, especially filibusters and legislative holds, were used broadly and repeatedly by all sides in the fight over the Chemical Weapons Convention. Eventually the Senate descended into "hostage taking" by using holds and filibusters against unrelated legislation as a means of leverage on the treaty. Finally, even in the high-stakes drama surrounding the Chemical Weapons Convention, Senator Helms successfully used procedural devices and personal prerogatives to block Senate consideration of the treaty for two and a half years, even though he could not get his own committee to support his position. Senator Lugar could form a majority on the committee that was supposed to have jurisdiction over the treaty, but he was deliberately excluded from the CWC task force by the Senate leadership.

While congressional Democrats overwhelmingly supported the treaty, Republicans were deeply divided over the issue. For those key Republican issue leaders on both sides of the treaty, issue loyalties superseded partisan and institutional ties. For the fence-sitters, however, political dynamics were much more significant. It was difficult for the president's congressional opposition to support the president on such a high-profile issue during an election season. Even treaty supporters felt reluctant to give the president a big win so soon before a presidential election. When Senator Dole, the Republican presidential candidate, came out against the treaty, the effort was certainly doomed. Few Republicans would be willing to oppose their presidential candidate six weeks before the election.

The CWC ratification process also epitomized the significance of cross-institutional linkages and spillover, in their positive and negative forms. The RCA issue illustrates the risks involved in an interagency process that forces some elements of the executive branch to take their grievances to sympathetic ears in Congress. A solid line of military support for the treaty was critical to passage, but the RCA issue gave treaty opponents a potent line of attack. Organizations such as the Veterans of Foreign Wars were slow to support the treaty because of the perception that it could endanger downed pilots by limiting the use of nonlethal weapons for self-protection. It was not until the executive branch shored up support for the treaty by revisiting the RCA issue and devising a more realistic and practical argument in favor of the treaty that such negative spillover could be contained.

While some of this spillover was harmful to the ratification process, informal, cross-institutional linkages were critical to formulating articles of ratification that would be acceptable to both branches. Following the aborted vote in September 1996, a small group of negotiators from the administration and key Senate staff conducted more than forty hours of negotiations to separate areas of disagreement into "understandings" to which the administration could agree and issues that would require the attention of the senators themselves. To make sure that protreaty senators who were not in the room would be on board when the vote came, Bell briefed Senator Lugar personally after each negotiating session. Without these relationships and the informal collaboration and negotiation they allowed, solutions to those problems would have been impossible.

Congress and the executive branch, however, did not act in a vacuum. Rather, the Chemical Weapons Convention is a striking example of the way that nongovernmental organizations operate within issue clusters. Organizations both for and against the treaty collaborated closely with like-minded members of Congress and the administration, parceling out roles and responsibilities to allow each element of the issue cluster to take advantage of its comparative advantage. Gaffney's Center for Security Policy, working closely with sympathetic Senate staffers and utilizing a powerful network of contacts and a fax machine, was largely responsible for derailing the first serious attempt at ratification in the fall of 1996. During round two, organizations supporting the treaty, such as the Henry L. Stimson Center, the Chemical Manufacturers Association, and Business Executives for National Security, seized the initiative by organizing media campaigns, engaging in broad-reaching public education, garnering important endorsements, and lobbying fence-sitting Republicans. These organizations were critical to the treaty's success.

In the almost four years it took to complete ratification of the Chemical Weapons Treaty, the treaty had gone from being what many considered a bipartisan "no-brainer" to one of the nastiest episodes of all-out foreign policy warfare in recent memory.[53] There is much to be learned. For example, the total fraying of relations between the State Department and the Senate Foreign Relations Committee made limited cooperation or even civil disagreement almost impossible. Locked in confrontation over the reorganization, normal processes of collaboration and negotiation were not operating effectively until after the 1996 election. Also, a more even-handed interagency process might have kept the RCA issue in check and prevented a number of early missteps. In addition, centralization of congressional negotiations in a single point of contact with credibility in both branches and more effective media and public outreach might have turned the tide earlier.

A more realistic assessment of the treaty's risks and benefits also would have built a broader coalition at an earlier stage in the process. If the administration had taken a more pragmatic approach to the treaty early in the process, round two might not have been necessary. Instead, conflicting signals over the priority of the treaty and a false confidence about the treaty's unimpeachable credentials allowed the treaty to drift until the opposition had solidified and political forces had found traction in the issue. Then, the administration used up considerable political capital to secure a floor vote, only to find out it did not have the votes for ratification.

Attempts at a "stealthy" strategy to slip the treaty through were misguided and naive.[54] Certainly, the executive branch cannot afford to treat treaty ratifications as anything less than major legislative initiatives that require a concerted and high-level effort by the executive. False starts and failed attempts only raise the bar further. The failed effort at CWC ratification in September 1996 put the administration and other treaty supporters at a significant procedural disadvantage and all but guaranteed the need for greater substantive concessions in round two. In today's climate, treaties and other major legislation will always require a full mobilization of resources inside and outside of the government, starting early in the process to optimize the chances of success. As one participant stated, "It is increasingly impossible to pass treaties. The supermajority required is a bar almost too high."[55]

The two-track approach, with more centralized coordination—preferably in the White House—provides a useful model for ratification efforts and other major legislation. Admittedly, this approach runs into big obstacles in the existing bureaucracies, which see this approach as a major incursion on their "turf." Such centralization makes it difficult for all of the interagency players to protect their equities in negotiations with Congress. Such powerful bureaucratic objections encourage the White House to provide the existing liaison and coordination mechanism an "opportunity to fail." This temptation needs to be avoided, since each failure makes success progressively more difficult to obtain.

The Clinton administration's subsequent track record on major treaties is decidedly mixed. On the one hand, the administration seemed to take some of the CWC lessons to heart in its effort to secure Senate ratification of enlargement of the North Atlantic Treaty Organization. Anxious to avoid another "near-death experience like the Chemical Weapons Convention," the president rehired his former National Security Council legislative affairs director, Jeremy Rosner, to lead the ratification effort and had him in place a full year before the historic vote.[56] Rosner sought and received the president's commitment to treat this ratification effort as a major administration priority and organized a centralized Office for NATO Ratification that reported to both the secretary of state and the national security adviser. Opponents to NATO expansion were late to organize and never captured momentum. The treaty passed overwhelmingly.

The more recent rejection of the Comprehensive Test Ban Treaty (CTBT), however, demonstrates just how short memories can be. President Clinton submitted the treaty to the Senate in September 1997, but the pact received only sporadic attention until the fall of 1999. With Senator Helms determined to keep the treaty off the Senate floor, Senate Democrats became increasingly vocal in their desires to debate the treaty. With the specter of additional filibusters and hostage taking on the rise, Senator Lott offered an agreement to debate the treaty on two weeks' notice, knowing that treaty opponents had the votes to defeat the resolution of ratification. Recognizing that they probably would not get another chance to consider the treaty this session, treaty proponents accepted the agreement.[57] When it became clear that the resolution would fail, the president and a bipartisan group of sixty-two senators asked to delay consideration of the treaty.[58] Nevertheless, the vote proceeded and on October 13 the Senate rejected the Comprehensive Test Ban Treaty by a vote of 51 to 48, resulting in "President Clinton's biggest foreign policy defeat on Capitol Hill."[59]

The test ban vote bears a strong resemblance to the first round of the CWC, only this time treaty opponents seemed to learn more than treaty supporters did. Stung by the CWC experience, CTBT opponents did not want to risk losing in a second round by allowing the treaty to "live to fight another day." This, in part, explains why these members were so reluctant to allow the treaty's supporters to withdraw the treaty when it was clear that the resolution to ratify it would not pass. Treaty supporters, forgetting that withdrawal of the treaty was a favor not a privilege, agreed to a unanimous consent agreement that left treaty opponents in the driver's seat and virtually guaranteed failure. The lessons of the CWC—among them, never regard treaties as anything less than a full-scale wave requiring broad-based outreach and centralized executive branch leadership—were stunningly absent.

SEVEN *The Way Ahead*

FOREIGN POLICY IN THE post–cold war era is profoundly complex, and so too are the institutions that share the responsibility to guide and manage America's foreign policy. Policymakers struggle within porous and fragmented institutions, where policy is driven more powerfully by clusters of like-minded individuals than by disciplined organizations. The nation's political parties face deep divisions over foreign policy and are unable to forge a coherent vision for the future of U.S. foreign policy. Congress is increasingly polarized along ideological lines, while traditional internationalist foreign policy lies astride a truncated political center. At the same time, the institutions have grown accustomed to hostility, conflict, and institutionalized partisanship that will not be readily dissipated readily. Finally, the "separate" branches of government are at some levels so intertwined that conflict over foreign policy is often as much intrabranch as interbranch. Today, policymakers of all forms—members of Congress and presidential appointees, congressional staffers and executive branch bureaucrats, even academics and advocates—are finding that not only the rules, but the game itself, has changed.

Implications for U.S. Foreign Policy

As the preceding chapters make clear, the complex and often troubled relationship between Congress and the executive branch over foreign policy defies simple explanations and convenient caricatures. The challenge of institutional weakness and individual power, the complexity of the informal procedural world, the potency of cross-institutional linkages, and the dominance of issued-based policy and politics define the reality of executive legislative relations in the 1990s and create a complex, nearly incoherent policy process. Many of these shifts have been under way for decades, deepening and expanding as the years passed, yet in many ways masked by cold war requirements that provided a structure to the policy process. The policy shocks of the 1990s have exposed and exacerbated these institutional dynamics, with considerable implications for U.S. foreign policy.

The policy shifts of the post–cold war period necessitate new structures and visions for the future. Today the United States relies on a national security architecture and foreign assistance structure that were designed to meet the needs of the cold war period. However, the lack of party or institutional discipline, combined with the force of informal influence and procedural tactics, greatly inhibits Congress's ability to form a majority in favor of internationalist trade and security policies. As a result, significant legislative reform will be difficult. Even modest legislative relief, such as that sought by the Brown amendment, requires powerful congressional champions and the commitment of much time and energy by senior executive branch officials.

However, individualized power and strong issue leaders have enhanced Congress's obstructive powers. While passing internationalist-leaning legislation may be difficult, coalitions of extremes and institutional hostility facilitate the passage of narrow, issue-based legislation, which often serves to limit executive flexibility or protect domestic interests. Faced with funding cuts, legislative restrictions, or lengthy delays in requested programs or activities, the executive branch has no choice but to take seriously the objections and concerns of individual members. The very strength of these obstructive powers makes them effective leverage against the executive branch and gives potency to the informal universe. The entire controversy over the Turkish frigates derived from this sort of individual and informal power. While both the Brown amendment and the Chemical Weapons Convention ultimately succeeded, their journey through the legislative process faced countless procedural roadblocks.

These obstructive powers, particularly in the Senate, have made it more and more difficult to move international agreements and treaties through the ratification process and to the floor of the Senate for a vote, let alone to secure the supermajority necessary for Senate approval. These difficulties are casting doubt on the credibility of U.S. negotiators and forcing a rethinking of the role of such agreements in U.S. foreign policy. Members of the executive branch need to accept the reality that treaty ratifications, especially in arms control, are major events requiring a long-term, sustained strategy of high-level, centralized engagement with Congress and the broader nongovernmental community.

Furthermore, as the perceived "stakes" associated with foreign policy decline, high-profile issues that capture the attention of the political leadership are vulnerable to political dynamics and linkages. It appears that these kinds of political linkages were prominent in the first round of the Chemical Weapons Convention when a looming presidential election made many Republicans reluctant to support a Democratic president on such a high-profile issue. More recently, the Comprehensive Test Ban Treaty fell victim to a similar dynamic, prompting Senator Chuck Hagel to explain, "This thing got snagged and dragged into the political swamp, and we couldn't rescue it."[1] In the Senate, ambassadorial and other nominees can face extraordinary delays as individual senators link the confirmation process to a host of unrelated issues. The House Republican leadership's decision to link the payment of U.S. arrears to the United Nations to controversial limitations on U.S. funding for family planning organizations that perform or advocate abortions (commonly referred to as the "Mexico City provision") is another example. That politically potent linkage triggered several presidential vetoes and tied up funding for the United Nations for more than four years. Foreign policy leaders, such as recently retired representative Lee Hamilton, have decried the expanded use of such linkages but to little avail.[2] Notably, however, such linkages are less evident in lower-profile issues, such as the Turkish frigates or the Brown amendment, where the controversy is generally confined to policy rather than politics.

In addition, both institutional dynamics and policy shifts of the post–cold war period contribute to a foreign policy that is far more issue based than vision based. A compelling grand strategy on the order of "containment" is not on the horizon. Organizational dynamics that favor issue leaders over institutional office holders complicate the government's ability to evaluate the trade-offs among different policy choices, especially when spearheaded by increasingly independent and effective interest groups and advocates. Issue leaders and issue clusters that operate independently of institutional and policy frameworks can exacerbate this splintering effect on foreign policy, especially when a single-issue constituency is aroused. For the foreseeable future, Congress and the executive will have little choice but to resolve their policy differences one issue at a time.

Finally, for both policy-related and institutional reasons, more new players than ever are participating in the struggle to direct U.S. foreign policy and national security. The State Department and the foreign affairs committees no longer dominate the scene. Today, foreign policy responsibilities are strewn across numerous federal departments and widely assorted congressional committees. The Departments of Treasury, Justice, and Defense, the Drug Enforcement Agency, even the Department of Health and Human Services are all vital in acting on issues such as the global financial system, counterterrorism, and the fight against illegal drugs. As these widely disparate federal entities expand their roles in U.S. foreign policy, so do each of their congressional oversight committees. Nongovernmental interest groups are now far more assertive on the world stage. Even state and local governments are moving into foreign policy. Consultation and coordination among these various entities are extremely difficult. Moreover, it is virtually impossible for Congress or the executive, let alone the government as a whole, to speak with one voice. U.S. diplomats charged with articulating U.S. policy and explaining these processes to their foreign counterparts face a daunting challenge.

Where Do We Go from Here?

As the previous chapters make clear, the potential for angry, disgruntled, or disaffected individuals in both branches of government to cause delay and controversy is considerable. A frustrated bureaucrat can trigger a firestorm with a single well-placed phone call. One motivated member of Congress can delay vital legislation, slash needed funding, or paralyze executive officials with a barrage of letters, requests, hearings, and reporting requirements. Institutional "gag orders" and punitive legislation often complete the downward spiral. Understandably, policymakers on both sides of the executive-legislative equation are preoccupied and frustrated with the state of their relationship.

There is, however, a positive face to these dynamics. Informal communication and dialogue can contribute to effective problem solving and conflict de-escalation. Armed with the advice of cross-institutional partners, policy advocates can shape programs and proposals to maximize support or better yet encourage an "in house" champion to assume ownership of the issue. Collaboration with strong issue leaders can help to shift the center of gravity on an issue and provide the counterweight necessary to effect positive change. Individuals can sidestep institutional and partisan differences to collaborate on a substantive agenda. Even those much-despised individual and procedural powers come in handy when it is the opposition's train that is being wrecked. This reality is the real message of the controversies over the Turkish ship transfers, the Brown amendment, and the Chemical Weapons Convention.

Dealing with these institutional realities in the post–cold war world is fraught with difficulties and challenges, but it is by no means hopeless. The fact is, Congress and the executive have been muddling along for quite a while and for now have avoided outright disaster. To paraphrase Mark Twain, reports of the complete demise of executive-legislative relations over foreign policy have been greatly exaggerated. Improvement, however, is necessary and possible. With a better understanding of the forces at work in executive-legislative relations, members of the foreign policy community—legislators, executive branch officials, academics—can help bring the foreign policy process into the twenty-first century. The institutional realities already described not only identify problems but also point out areas of potential improvement.

What Not to Do

For starters, calls to reclaim executive authority and return to some nostalgic heyday of congressional deference on foreign policy are unrealistic, unwise, and unnecessary. First, Congress has neither the willingness nor the ability to relinquish its ability to influence foreign policy. Without the rise of a major new threat to the nation's security to galvanize support and subdue congressional intervention, this is unlikely to change. Second, while congressional influence over foreign policy has expanded significantly since World War II, the president still has the power to act independently in foreign policy, power that the president often exercises. As seen in the matter of the Turkish frigates, presidential reluctance to act unilaterally has more to do with a desire to avoid punitive measures, political controversy, and damaged relations than with Congress's overt ability to stop the president from pursuing a course of action. Moreover, today much of the concern lies in what Congress does not do, as well as what it does. It is Congress's failure to act in areas such as foreign affairs funding, UN arrearages, or free trade agreements that prompts fears of an anti-internationalist Congress. How does an institution cede the power to do nothing?

Neither is there much to be gained from calls for "united government" or renewed bipartisanship as the solution to the heightened conflict over foreign policy. In the 1990s, partisan ties tend to divide as much as they unite. Our limited experiences with united government also suggest such arrangements provide little guaranteed agreement over foreign affairs. Moreover, deepening ideological polarization continues to reduce the prospect for increased bipartisanship except as "coalitions of extremes," which usually are hostile to traditional, internationalist foreign policy interests. Both parties are pulled in unhelpful directions by an ideologically extreme base. Greater bipartisanship of the traditional variety will require the resurrection of the political center. Finally, by focusing on partisan solutions, both branches risk dragging foreign policy issues unnecessarily into the political sphere, where the risk of political and domestic linkages is higher.

Finally, by dismissing the complexities and problems of executive-legislative relations and foreign policy as simply an absence of leadership, many observers and foreign policy practitioners fail to understand that these institutional realities are endemic, not simply a function of a particular administration or congressional leadership. No substitute exists for effective leadership, but indiscriminate calls for higher and higher levels of engagement on more and more topics amounts to little more than dumping an ever-increasing number of issues on the presidential plate. Today's institutional realities demand that the president focus on setting and prioritizing foreign policy goals as well as building support for them, all the while saving room and time for genuine emergencies and vital legislation. The same holds true for the Speaker of the House and the Senate majority leader. Moreover, issues that must be resolved by the president and the congressional leadership are far more likely to become entangled in domestic politics and partisan bickering, as these top policymakers strain to balance their ideological, partisan, and issue loyalties.

What Can Be Done?

There is no "solution" to the challenges at hand. Still, problems can be managed and perhaps mitigated. The following steps would help:

—*Master the informal universe.* Executive branch policymakers need to become much more effective masters of the informal universe. Procedural and informal powers often favor members of Congress and their staff partly because they are more adept at its use and partly because the threat of retaliation is not easily matched by the executive. Far too few executive branch policymakers understand the formal legislative process, let alone the informal process through which so much interaction between the branches occurs. Understanding the process and the motivations of the various parties helps to develop creative solutions to problems. As in all facets of policymaking, knowledge, even of the procedural variety, is power. Learning the system is important for new administrations, which tend to scoff at these rituals and routines as excessively bureaucratic. New administrations need to select a foreign policy team with strong procedural skills and experience in the executive-legislative arena and work closely with Congress to streamline the nomination and confirmation process. Otherwise, a new president is likely to get "outplayed" by his or her congressional counterparts or pay a significant price before finally heeding the lessons of the informal game.

—*Understand the difference between the ocean and the waves and act accordingly.* The goal is to maximize the number of issues handled informally and quietly among the foreign policy professionals and minimize the number of high-profile institutional clashes, or waves. Ocean issues usually require very different strategies and solutions than waves. Issues in the ocean are usually best handled as "inside jobs." Public admonitions tend to lock in positions and escalate the conflict. Many problems arising from either branch can be deflected by early, informal interventions. Contrary to the instincts of many policymakers, handling issues at higher and higher levels is not always the better way. High-profile and public issues are much more vulnerable to broader political dynamics and are often subject to trading and hostage taking. Issues that can stay in the informal universe are far more likely to be resolved within a community of foreign policy professionals.

Issues that are mishandled in the informal universe risk turning into waves, genuine institutional clashes over policy and substantive legislation. Given the vulnerable base of support for many traditional facets of foreign policy and the increased linkages between foreign affairs and domestic issues, the chance of a successful resolution diminishes sharply once the institutions are locked in combat. That said, treating a major foreign policy issue with anything less than the seriousness it deserves is equally damaging. False starts and failed efforts almost always make the subsequent attempts more difficult. Both success and failure have a momentum of their own. Waves need to be addressed publicly through a broad public relations campaign and privately through "inside track" negotiations. These issues require the full mobilization of resources and the intense involvement of the highest levels of the executive. Treaty ratifications, given the sixty-seven-vote supermajority they require, are nearly always waves.

—*Promote and expand informal communication.* Executive-legislative conflict tends to produce an instinct within the executive branch to clamp down broadly on informal communication by imposing gag orders and prohibiting any communication with Congress that is not expressly approved and monitored by legislative advisers. Such efforts are usually counterproductive. Gag orders have more impact on the positive aspects of spillover—collaboration and early problem solving—than they do on determined efforts to transfer interagency disputes into the congressional arena. Officials who want to bring their concerns to congressional attention will find a way, either through private conversations or through the use of nongovernmental entities and interest groups as "water carriers." With few exceptions, more communication, not less, is the answer to conflict. This does not mean that government agencies should dismantle their legislative liaison operations and permit unbridled freelancing. It does mean that these offices should encourage, but be well informed about, strong channels of communication and informal problem solving.

—*Implement regular presidential and other senior-level consultations.* "Don't just call when you want something." This long-standing advice from legislative advisers to policymakers bears repeating. Crisis-driven, episodic meetings and consultations generate little good will and reinforce the dominance of single-issue constituencies. Informal communication is great, but it is no substitute for a president who cares and genuinely consults. The challenges to effective consultations in an environment dominated by individualized power and issues leaders are sizable. Nevertheless, the president and other senior officials and advisers need to demonstrate consistent, broad-based interest in foreign policy and communicate this attentiveness on a regular basis directly with members of Congress. Routine, informal meetings between the president and pertinent congressional leaders can contribute toward a more integrated approach to foreign policy and build residual good will for the inevitable crises. It would also strengthen the institutional position of the committee leadership members, especially if such consultations coincided with a strengthening of the foreign affairs committees and their chairmen. It is impossible to expect Congress to be more interested and consistent in foreign policy than the president.

—*Encourage modest reforms of procedural powers.* Congress, particularly the leadership, can have a resounding effect on restoring a sense of credibility and fairness to this process. It is up to the leadership to curtail the exponential growth in the use of filibusters, threatened filibusters, and holds. Major reforms, while perhaps necessary, are unrealistic. A few minor changes, intended to signal that the use of these devices as de facto "vetoes" will warrant greater scrutiny, are appropriate. Senators Ron Wyden (D-Ore.) and Charles Grassley (R-Iowa) have sponsored legislation that would modify Senate rules, requiring "senators who have placed holds to publicly reveal that action, and their identity, within 48 hours."[3] This provision, which was successfully attached to the fiscal year 1999 defense authorization bill but did not survive conference, could help to reduce the more debilitating effects of holds. Even more modest reforms, such as limiting the number or days of holds or filibusters during the last few weeks of the session, would sharply reduce their veto power and could be accomplished through the agreement of the majority and minority leaders.

—*Recognize the longer-term implications of short-term decisions.* Negotiation and compromise are essential elements of effective executive-legislative relations. Nevertheless, both sides need to keep in mind that these "deals" often have a long life span. Legislation creates binding requirements not only for the president and Congress that agree to it but also for subsequent foreign policy leaders who may labor under new and changed circumstances. As with the Pressler amendment and other proliferation sanctions, both Congress and the president often come to regret legislation that is unduly rigid and inflexible. Sunset provisions and waivers are important ways that today's foreign policy practitioners can ensure that future leaders need not labor under outdated and anachronistic requirements. The executive branch also needs to exercise caution as negotiations intended to solve short-term problems often result in procedural commitments (such as the complex agreements on arms transfers) that can last for decades, developing a sort of institutional momentum that can far outlast their usefulness. That said, the executive should not simply attempt to disregard long-standing informal agreements. Such a break in the trust between the branches would produce long-term repercussions and probably result in legislative requirements for matters previously handled through informal agreements.

—*Revitalize the authorization committees.* One of the most important things Congress could do would be to revitalize the foreign affairs authorization committees, which have grown more irrelevant during the past decade. Although there is no quick fix for this problem, improvement is not impossible. The first step would be for the House and Senate leadership to encourage strong committee leadership and a reinvigorated chairmanship. Both the House and the Senate need strong foreign affairs leaders with the power to legislate and the ability to command a majority within their respective body. As occurred in the fight over the Chemical Weapons Convention, Senator Helms is often forced to make extreme use of his personal and prerogative powers because he cannot command a majority within his committee, let alone the Senate as a whole. Strong committees and strong chairmen will provide the necessary counterweight to the growing power of issue leaders, since their interests and equities will naturally cover a broader range of issues.

The leadership also needs to recommit to the authorization process, providing an appropriate vehicle for foreign affairs legislation that now crops up all over the place. First, authorization on an appropriations bill must be a "last resort" rather than a convenient way to avoid two votes on foreign aid. Second, the leadership must resist the use of foreign affairs legislation as the dumping ground for nongermane or politically loaded amendments. The faltering of the State Department authorization process over the past five years results almost exclusively from its linkage to the politically volatile abortion issue. A commitment to the authorization process would go a long way toward reversing the impression among many members that foreign affairs is a dead-end assignment and a political liability. Lawmakers want to legislate, and a committee that cannot pass legislation will always struggle to attract high-caliber members. Rebuilding the committees would also help to cultivate the next generation of foreign affairs leadership in Congress.

—*Bring back the junket.* New members of Congress are not coming into office with the same level of military or foreign policy interest and experience as their predecessors. At the same time, the system is placing more and more power to affect foreign policy, through action or inaction, into their hands. Educating members about the "on-the-ground realities" of U.S. foreign policy is more important than ever, yet the "boondoggle" stigma attached to foreign travel is keeping members, especially the newer ones, home during congressional recesses. For all of their bad press, these trips provide an extraordinary opportunity to educate members on foreign affairs. More opportunities for education and information must be targeted at younger, newer members. Understandably, these members do not want to withstand the withering "junket attacks" that appear in Al Kamen's "In the Loop" column in the *Washington Post* on a routine basis. Nor does it inspire members' interest in foreign affairs when House Majority Leader Dick Armey (R-Tex.) feels compelled to boast to reporters that he has not "traveled outside the United States since 1986."[4]

Unfortunately, no one is offering a counterweight to these political attacks. The executive branch can play a role here. Rather than complaining about congressional delegations, the executive branch should encourage substantive fact-finding missions and speak out for their importance in speeches, op-eds, and other exchanges with the media.

—*Centralize legislative relations for high-priority or cross-cutting issues in the White House.* Individual agencies and departments must preserve the right to take the lead on issues of their jurisdiction and involving their oversight committees, but the White House must provide centralized leadership and coordination on cross-cutting or high-priority issues. Only a more centralized and less bureaucratized authority can supervise the broad outreach campaigns now needed for major legislative efforts, such as treaty ratifications or trade legislation. In interviews, congressional staff consistently pointed out the importance of this centralized coordination in round two of the Chemical Weapons Convention and in the expansion vote for the North Atlantic Treaty Organization. The executive must act before disaster has already struck.

—*Be realistic.* The interagency process can be a very good predictor of congressional reaction to a given policy issue. Either because of policy affinity or because problems have "spilled over," different elements within the legislative branch are likely to replicate the positions taken by different elements of the executive. The interagency process therefore can be a useful strategic tool in forecasting and responding to congressional objections. Similarly, contentious and hostile interagency battles are almost always replicated in similar intensity once the issue moves to Capitol Hill.

Efforts to forcefully impose a solution on the interagency process and then present a fait accompli to Congress (usually on a very short timeline) are unrealistic and almost never work. The executive simply refights the same issue, but this time in a broader conflict. Rather than forcing all elements of the bureaucracy to toe some heavily scripted "party line" (which they promptly abandon in private, informal discussions), it is better to frame alternate views, explain trade-offs, and justify how an issue's "pros" outweigh its "cons." Information gleaned from the informal universe is less powerful when it is consistent with public and formal positions. Then leave sufficient time for consultation and debate. Executive branch officials will complain that they do not have time for this approach. While the assertion is probably true, the fact is that the choice is not always theirs to make. As the examples in this book make clear, false starts and failed strategies can result in months and even years of delay over which the executive has no control. Being more realistic from the beginning will save time and effort in the end.

—*Fight fire with fire.* The best way to counter a powerful issue leader is to find an alternative champion, build a coalition of like-minded individuals from both government and the nongovernmental community, and shift the center of gravity. Only another champion can counter the procedural and informal powers of a determined issue leader. Counterholds and legislative hostage taking should not be used capriciously, but sometimes these tactics are the only way to combat the excessive use of individual power.

Moreover, it takes an issue cluster to beat an issue cluster. Media pot shots and fax attacks cannot go unanswered. Yet without the information sharing, early warning and rapid-reaction capabilities of an issue cluster, the response is often too little, too late. This process is critical for high-profile issues, such as the Chemical Weapons Convention, and for lower-profile issues such as sanctions relief for Pakistan. In the bigger picture, the president and other advocates of strong internationalist foreign policy must raise the political salience of U.S. foreign policy. As long as low risk and an inattentive public make it "cost free" for individuals and groups to pursue narrow agendas at the expense of the national interests, change will be slow in coming.

Notes

Chapter One

1. Key works in the debate over the appropriate roles of Congress and the executive branch in foreign and defense policy include Arthur M. Schlesinger, Jr., *The Imperial Presidency* (Houghton Mifflin, 1973); Thomas M. Franck and Edward Weisband, *Foreign Policy by Congress* (Oxford University Press, 1979); Warren Christopher, "Ceasefire between the Branches: A Compact in Foreign Affairs," *Foreign Affairs*, vol. 60 (Summer 1983), pp. 989–1005; John G. Tower, "Congress versus the President: The Formulation and Implementation of American Foreign Policy," *Foreign Affairs* (Winter 1981–82), pp. 229–46; Thomas Franck, ed., *The Tethered Presidency: Congressional Restraints on Foreign Policy* (New York University Press, 1981); L. Gordon Crovitz and Jeremy Rabkin, eds., *The Fettered Presidency: Legal Constraints on the Executive Branch* (Washington: American Enterprise Institute, 1989); Gordon S. Jones and John Marini, eds., *The Imperial Congress: Crisis in the Separation of Powers* (Pharos Books, 1988); James L. Sundquist, *The Decline and Resurgence of Congress* (Brookings, 1981); Dick Cheney, "Congressional Overreaching in Foreign Policy," in Robert A. Goldwin and Robert A. Licht, eds., *Foreign Policy and the Constitution* (Washington: American Enterprise Institute, 1990); and Stephen R. Weissman, *A Culture of Deference: Congress's Failure of Leadership in Foreign Policy* (Basic Books, 1995). For a useful summary of literature on Congress and foreign policy see James M. Lindsay and Randall B. Ripley, "Foreign and Defense Policy in Congress: A Research Agenda for the 1990s," *Legislative Studies Quarterly*, vol. 17 (August 1992), pp. 417–49.

2. Michael Clough, "Grass-Roots Policy-making: Say Good-Bye to the 'Wise Men'," *Foreign Affairs*, vol. 73 (January-February, 1994), p. 2.

3. Steven Pearlstein, "On Trade, U.S. Retreating into Globalphobia," *Washington Post*, December 8, 1997, p. A1. This front-page article is typical of the sweeping conclusions that these high-profile events generate. Pearlstein describes the decision to strip funding for the International Monetary Fund and the defeat of "fast-track" legislation as "the latest illustration of . . . a retreat from the internationalist consensus that has governed U.S. economic policy for the last 50 years."

4. Samuel R. Berger, speech before the Council on Foreign Relations, New York City, October 21, 1999, as reprinted in the *Washington Post*, October 31, 1999, p. B3.

5. An extensive 1997 study by the Pew Research Center for People and the Press found that foreign policy barely appears in any list of the public's concerns or priorities—which are overwhelmingly domestic. Pew Research Center for the People and the Press, *America's Place in the World, II* (Washington, 1997), p. 6.

Chapter Two

1. Richard E. Neustadt, *Presidential Power: The Politics of Leadership* (John Wiley and Sons, 1969), p. 33. Emphasis in original.

2. Neustadt, *Presidential Power*, pp. 33–34.

3. Interview with administration official, April 4, 1998.

4. Roger H. Davidson, "The Presidency and Congressional Time," in James A. Thurber, ed., *Rivals for Power: Presidential-Congressional Relations* (Washington: CQ Press, 1996), p. 29.

5. James M. Lindsay, *Congress and the Politics of U.S. Foreign Policy* (Johns Hopkins University Press, 1994), p. 26.

6. A useful summary of congressional reforms during the 1970s can be found in Leroy N. Rieselbach, *Congressional Reform: The Changing Modern Congress* (Washington: CQ Press, 1994), pp. 45–93.

7. Barbara Sinclair, *Unorthodox Lawmaking: New Legislative Processes in the U.S. Congress* (Washington: CQ Press, 1997), pp. 75–77.

8. Sinclair, *Unorthodox Lawmaking*, p. 97.

9. A useful analysis of the reforms of the 1994 Gingrich revolution can be found in John H. Aldrich and David W. Rohde, "The Transition to Republican Rule in the House: Implications for Theories of Congressional Politics," *Political Science Quarterly*, vol. 112 (Winter 1997-1998), pp. 541–67. See also Sinclair, *Unorthodox Lawmaking*, pp. 96–100.

10. Interview with administration official, June 21, 1999.

11. Interview with administration official, June 21, 1999.

12. Lee H. Hamilton, "The Role of the Congress in U.S. Foreign Policy," speech before the Center for Strategic and International Studies, November 19, 1998, Washington.

13. Interview with Defense Department official, June 14, 1999. See also "Legislative Summary: Appropriations," *Congressional Quarterly Weekly Report*, November 14, 1998, p. 3203.

14. Interview with administration official, June 14, 1999.

15. See Morton H. Halperin, *Bureaucratic Politics and Foreign Policy* (Brookings, 1974).

16. Rieselbach, *Congressional Reform*, p. 55.

17. Aldrich and Rohde, "The Transition to Republican Rule in the House," pp. 541–67.

18. Interview with House staffer, June 23, 1999.

19. Interview with administration official, June 21, 1999.

20. Interview with House staffer, February 8, 1998.

21. Interview with Defense Department official, June 14, 1999.

22. Interview with administration official, June 21, 1999.

23. According to the 1997 study by the Pew Research Center for People and the Press, varying majorities of Americans (55 percent to 66 percent) say that events in Europe, Asia, Mexico, and Canada have little or no personal relevance to them. In addition, public attitudes are not well informed. Sixty-three percent of the public supported expansion of the North Atlantic Treaty Organization, but only 10 percent could name any one of the three countries to be admitted. Only 8 percent of public respondents could answer three basic foreign policy questions—name the president of Russia, identify one of the three countries to be admitted to NATO, and identify the Canadian province threatening to secede. *America's Place in the World, II*, p. 6.

24. Interview with House Republican staffer, February 8, 1998.

25. Interview with Michael Van Dusen, February 8, 1998.

26. Miles A. Pomper, "The New Faces of Foreign Policy," *Congressional Quarterly Weekly Report*, November 28, 1998, p. 3203. The seven subcommittee chairmen were Chuck Hagel, International Economic Policy, Export and Trade Promotion; Gordon H. Smith, European Affairs; Craig Thomas, East Asian and Pacific Affairs; Bill Frist, African Affairs; Rod Grams, International Operations; Paul Coverdell, Western Hemisphere, Peace Corps, Narcotics and Terrorism; Sam Brownback, Near Eastern and South Asian Affairs.

27. Helen Dewar, "Farming Locally, Thinking Globally; As Trade Booms, Midwesterners Fight Isolationism in the GOP," *Washington Post*, April 21, 1998, p. A1.

28. Senator Pat Roberts, remarks before the Kansas Press Association, Manhattan, Kansas, April 10, 1998.

29. Helen Dewar, "Senate Rejects Test Ban Treaty: Nuclear Pact Fails 51 to 48 as GOP Deals Clinton Major Defeat," *Washington Post*, October 14, 1999, p. A1. As this article points out, "Not since the Treaty of Versailles to establish the League of Nations after World War I had the Senate formally rejected a

major arms control accord, although it has delayed action to avert defeat and has occasionally rejected treaties on other subjects. The Senate last rejected a treaty in 1983."

30. Cecil V. Crabb, Jr., and Pat M. Holt, *Invitation to Struggle: Congress, the President and Foreign Policy,* 4th ed. (Washington: CQ Press, 1992), pp. 175–76. I. M. Destler, Leslie H. Gelb and Anthony Lake, *Our Own Worst Enemy: The Unmaking of American Foreign Policy* (Simon and Schuster, 1984) p. 132.

31. A number of scholars have sought to examine the varying ways that Congress influences policy. See, for example, Robert Gilmour and Alexis A. Halley, eds., *Who Makes Public Policy?: The Struggle for Control between Congress and the Executive* (Chatham House Publishers, 1994); Thurber, *Rivals for Power,* pp. 1–18; Walter J. Oleszek, *Congressional Procedures and the Policy Process* (Washington: CQ Press, 1996); Randall B. Ripley and James M. Lindsay, *Congress Resurgent: Foreign and Defense Policy on Capitol Hill* (University of Michigan Press, 1993); Lindsay, *Congress and the Politics of U.S. Foreign Policy;* Thomas E. Mann, *A Question of Balance: The President, the Congress and Foreign Policy* (Brookings, 1990).

32. Lindsay, *Congress and the Politics of U.S. Foreign Policy,* p. 132.

33. Interview with Defense Security Assistance Agency official, October 19, 1998.

34. Richard Grimmett, "Arms Sales: Congressional Review Process," *CRS Report for Congress,* No. 92-914F (Washington: Congressional Research Service, December 1992), p. 1.

35. Interview with administration official, April 9, 1998.

36. Interview with Defense Security Assistance Agency official, October 19, 1998.

37. Sinclair, *Unorthodox Lawmaking,* pp. 38–42.

38. Ibid., pp. 46–50.

39. For a more detailed explanation of Senate floor procedures, including the process for filibusters and cloture, see Oleszek, *Congressional Procedures,* pp. 206–07, 249–56.

40. Sarah A. Binder and Steven S. Smith, *Politics or Principle?: Filibustering in the United States Senate* (Brookings, 1997), pp. 9–11.

41. Charles McC. Mathias, "Gridlock, Greedlock or Democracy?" *Washington Post,* June 27, 1994, p. A21.

42. Oleszek, *Congressional Procedures,* pp. 206–07.

43. Binder and Smith, *Politics or Principle?,* pp. 10–12.

44. Jessica Lee, "Old Senate Tactic Has a Hold on Holbrooke," *USA Today,* July 15, 1999, p. 7A.

45. Lee Hamilton and Michael van Dusen, "Making the Separation of Powers Work," *Foreign Affairs,* vol. 57 (Fall 1978), p. 22.

46. Hamilton and Van Dusen, "Making the Separation of Powers Work," p. 22, note 1.

47. Interview with Department of State official, April 9, 1998.

48. David R. Mayhew, *Divided We Govern: Party Control, Lawmaking and Investigations, 1946-1990* (Yale University Press, 1991). Mayhew's analysis of 267 significant laws finds "united government" provides little benefit in terms of the enactment of important legislation.

49. Eric Pianin, "Some in GOP Don't Buy the 'Contract'; Critics Compare Gingrich Plan with Faults of Supply-Side Economics (chart summary of Contract)," *Washington Post*, September 30, 1994, p. A10.

50. Pat Towell, "House Votes to Sharply Rein in U.S. Peacekeeping Expenses," *Congressional Quarterly Weekly Report*, February 18, 1995, pp. 535–37.

51. U.S. Department of State, *Dispatch*, June 5, 1995, p. 486.

52. Pat Towell, "Rebellious House Republicans Help Crush Defense Bill," *Congressional Quarterly Weekly Report*, September 30, 1995, pp. 3013–16.

53. James L. Sundquist, ed., *Beyond Gridlock?: Prospects for Governance in the Clinton Years and After* (Brookings, 1993), p. 25.

54. Mann, *A Question of Balance*, p. 28.

55. Robert D. Reischauer, "Budget Policy under United Government: A Case Study," in James L. Sundquist, ed., *Back to Gridlock? Governance in the Clinton Years* (Brookings, 1995), p. 20.

56. David Hosansky, "IMF Contribution Finds Enemies across the Political Spectrum," *Congressional Quarterly Weekly Report*, January 31, 1998, pp. 232–35; and David Hosansky, "Request for Billions for IMF Fund Highlights Debate over Bailouts," *Congressional Quarterly Weekly Report*, January 10, 1998, pp. 64–65.

57. Pat Towell, "Senate Approves Three Nations for Membership in NATO," *Congressional Quarterly Weekly Report*, May 2, 1998, p. 1172.

58. Sarah Binder, "The Disappearing Political Center: Congress and the Incredible Shrinking Middle," *Brookings Review* (Fall 1996), pp. 36–39.

59. David Hosansky, "The GOP's House Divided: Social Activists vs. Business," *Congressional Quarterly Weekly Report*, May 30, 1998, p. 1447.

60. Senator Pat Roberts, remarks before the Kansas Press Association, Manhattan, Kansas, April 10, 1998.

61. Miles A. Pomper, "The Religious Right's Foreign Policy Revival," *Congressional Quarterly Weekly Report*, May 9, 1998, pp. 1209–10.

62. Miles Pomper, "GOP's Abortion Curb Advances as House Democrats Fall Back," *Congressional Quarterly Weekly Report*, March 26, 1998, pp. 828–29.

63. Miles A. Pomper, "Clinton Uncaps Veto Pen as State Department Bill Clears," *Congressional Quarterly Weekly Report*, May 2, 1998, pp. 1167–68.

64. Hugh Heclo, "Issue Networks and the Executive Establishment," in Anthony King, ed., *The New American Political System* (Washington: American Enterprise Institute, 1978), p. 116.

65. Christine DeGregorio, *Network of Champions: Leadership, Access, and Advocacy in the U.S. House of Representatives* (University of Michigan Press, 1997), p. 17.

66. DeGregorio, *Network of Champions*, p. 4.

67. Robert S. Gilmour and Eric Minkoff, "Producing a Reliable Weapons System: AMRAAM," in Robert Gilmour and Alexis A. Halley, eds., *Who Makes Public Policy?: The Struggle for Control between Congress and the Executive* (Chatham House Publishers, 1994), pp. 201–03.

68. Interview with House staffer, April 8, 1998.

69. Paula Stern challenged the separateness of U.S. domestic and foreign policies in 1979 in Paula Stern, *Water's Edge: Domestic Politics and the Making of American Foreign Policy* (Greenwood Press, 1979).

70. Paul Overberg and Shana Gruskin, "105th Congress: A Closer Look," *USA Today*, November 7, 1996, p. 6A.

Chapter Three

1. Hugh Heclo, "Issue Networks and the Executive Establishment" in Anthony King, ed., *The New American Political System* (Washington: American Enterprise Institute, 1978) pp. 87–124; Douglass Cater, *Power in Washington: A Critical Look at Today's Struggle to Govern in the Nation's Capitol* (Random House, 1964); Hank C. Jenkins-Smith and Paul A. Sabatier, eds., *Policy Change and Learning: An Advocacy Coalition Approach* (Westview Press, 1993). For a summary of much of the subsystem literature see also Michael Howlett and M. Ramesh, *Studying Public Policy: Policy Cycles and Policy Subsystems* (Oxford University Press, 1995), pp. 122–35.

2. To avoid the negative connotations associated with many of the characterizations of this phenomenon already in play (issue networks, advocacy coalitions, and so on), I refer to these informal groupings of likeminded policymakers from Congress, the executive and nongovernmental entities as "issue clusters."

3. James A. Thurber, "An Introduction to Presidential-Congressional Rivalry," in James A. Thurber, ed., *Rivals for Power: Presidential-Congressional Relations* (Washington: CQ Press, 1996), p. 3.

4. Edward S. Corwin, *The President: Offices and Powers 1787-1957*, 4th rev. ed. (New York University Press, 1957), p. 171.

5. U.S. Constitution, art. 1, sec. 8, 9; art. 2, sec. 2.

6. Douglas J. Bennett, "Congress in Foreign Policy: Who Needs It?" *Foreign Affairs*, vol. 57 (Fall 1978), p. 41.

7. Interview with Department of Defense official, June 14, 1999.

8. Thomas E. Mann, ed., *A Question of Balance: The President, the Congress, and Foreign Policy* (Brookings, 1990), p. 28.

9. Interview with executive branch official, September 24, 1998.

10. Miles A. Pomper, "House Shies Away from Conflict with Clinton over War Powers," *Congressional Quarterly Weekly Report*, March 21, 1998, pp. 760–61.

11. James M. Lindsay, *Congress and the Politics of U.S. Foreign Policy* (Johns Hopkins University Press, 1994), p. 6.

12. Interview with Department of Defense official, February 19, 1998.

13. Interview with Department of Defense official, February 19, 1998.

14. For a more detailed case study on peacekeeping policy and funding early in the Clinton administration, see Jeremy Rosner's *The New Tug-of-War: Congress, the Executive and National Security* (Washington: Carnegie Endowment for International Peace,1995), pp. 65–91.

15. Ibid., p. 83 (emphasis in original).

16. Ibid., pp. 86, 90–91.

17. Interview with Michael Van Dusen, minority staff director, House International Relations Committee, February 8, 1998.

18. Interviews with House staffer, February 8, 1998, and administration official, April 9, 1998. See also Donna Cassata, "Opponents of Certifying Mexico as Drug Ally Face Uphill Battle," *Congressional Quarterly Weekly Report*, March 7, 1998, pp. 575–76.

19. Interview with Jeremy Rosner, July 23, 1998.

20. Interview with Department of Defense official, February 19, 1998.

21. Robert S. Gilmour and Eric Minkoff, "Producing a Reliable Weapons System: AMRAAM," in Robert Gilmour and Alexis A. Halley, eds., *Who Makes Public Policy?: The Struggle for Control between Congress and the Executive* (Chatham House Publishers, 1994) p. 203.

22. Gilmour and Minkoff, "Producing a Reliable Weapons System," p. 203.

23. Nina M. Serafino, "Peacekeeping: Issues of U.S. Military Involvement," CRS Issue Brief No. 94040 (Washington: Congressional Research Service, updated July 26, 1999), p. 4.

24. James M. Lindsay, "Congress, Foreign Policy and the New Institutionalism," *International Studies Quarterly*, vol. 38 (June 1994), pp. 281–304.

25. G. Calvin MacKenzie, "Resolving Policy Differences: Foreign Aid and Human Rights," in Robert Gilmour and Alexis A. Halley, eds., *Who Makes Public Policy?: The Struggle for Control between Congress and the Executive* (Chatham House Publishers, 1994), pp. 272–73.

26. James M. Lindsay, "The State Department Complex after the Cold War," in Randall B. Ripley and James M. Lindsay, eds., *U.S. Foreign Policy after the Cold War*, (University of Pittsburgh Press, 1997), pp. 74–105.

27. MacKenzie, "Resolving Policy Differences," pp. 274–75.

28. Ibid.

29. Ibid., p. 282.

30. James Lindsay, "Congress and Foreign Policy: Why the Hill Matters," *Political Science Quarterly*, vol. 107 (Winter 1992), pp. 613–16.

31. Gilmour and Minkoff, "Producing a Reliable Weapons System," p. 211.

32. Interviews with Department of Defense officials, April 1, 1998, and interview with Department of State official, July 1998.

33. James Lindsay describes the "belief that the electoral connection makes members of Congress inherently irresponsible on foreign policy" as the "electoral fallacy." Lindsay, *Congress and the Politics of U.S. Foreign Policy*.

34. Christine DeGregorio, *Network of Champions: Leadership, Access and Advocacy in the U.S. House of Representatives* (University of Michigan Press, 1997), pp. 118–19.

35. Hugh Heclo, "Issue Networks and the Executive Establishment," in Anthony King, ed., *The New American Political System* (Washington: American Enterprise Institute, 1978), p. 116.

36. Interview with administration official, June 17, 1999. For background on the Nunn-Lugar problem and its struggles with congressional support, see Jason D. Ellis and Todd Perry, "Nunn-Lugar's Unfinished Agenda," *Arms Control Today*, vol. 27 (October 1997), pp. 14–22.

37. Jody Williams, coordinator, International Campaign to Ban Landmines, Nobel lecture, Oslo, December 10, 1997. As of December 31, 1999 the committee is composed of more than 1,300 organizations from seventy-five countries. There are now 136 signatories to the convention and, it has been ratified by forty countries.

38. Pat Towell, "Supporters of Land Mine Ban Step Up Pressure on Clinton," *Congressional Quarterly Weekly Report*, August 30, 1997, pp. 2045–47.

39. Williams, Nobel lecture.

40. Jessica T. Mathews, "Power Shift," *Foreign Affairs*, vol. 76 (January-February 1997), p. 54.

41. Margaret E. Keck and Kathryn Sikkink, *Activists beyond Borders: Advocacy Networks in International Politics* (Cornell University Press, 1998), pp. 12–13.

42. Mathews, "Power Shift," p. 55.

43. Office of Senator Tom Daschle, "Daschle, Lott Appoint Bipartisan Senate Task Force on Use of Economic Sanctions," press release, June 26, 1998.

44. Carroll J. Doherty, "Proliferation of Sanctions Creates a Tangle of Good Intentions," *Congressional Quarterly Weekly Report*, September 13, 1997, p. 2113.

45. For an analysis of the use of sanctions in the post–cold war period see Richard N. Haass, ed., *Economic Sanctions and American Diplomacy* (New York: Council on Foreign Relations Press, 1998).

46. Interview with former administration official, July 23, 1998.

47. Miles Pomper, "Second-Guessing Sanctions: The Price of Pressure," *Congressional Quarterly Weekly Report*, August 15, 1998, pp. 2237–40; and Miles Pomper, "Stoked by Farm Interests, Anti-Sanctions Movement Builds in Both Chambers," *Congressional Quarterly Weekly Report*, March 27, 1999, p. 767.

48. Senator Jesse Helms, "What Sanctions Epidemic? U.S. Business' Curious Crusade," *Foreign Affairs*, vol. 78 (January-February 1999), pp. 2–8.

Chapter Four

1. Umit Enginsoy and Philip Finnegan, "Turkey Plans Navy Upgrade with Frigate Transfers, Buys," *Defense News*, August 14, 1995, p. 10.

2. Statistics referenced in "Protect Statecraft Tools," *Defense News*, November 6, 1995, p. 18, and also discussed in an interview with Department of Defense official, April 1, 1998.

3. Interview with Department of Defense official, April 1, 1998.

4. Interview with Department of Defense official, April 1, 1998.

5. Interviews with Department of Defense official, April 1, 1998, and with House staffer, February 8, 1998.

6. Phillip Finnegan, "Congress May Sink Frigate Grants," *Defense News*, October 23, 1995, p. 3.

7. Interviews with Department of Defense official, April 1, 1998, and with House staffer, February 8, 1998. See also Finnegan, "Congress May Sink Frigate Grants," p. 3.

8. *National Defense Authorization Act for Fiscal Year 1996*, Conference Report HR 104-406, sec. 1012, 104 Cong. 2 sess. (1995).

9. Interviews with Department of Defense official, April 1, 1998.

10. Interview with Department of Defense official, April 1, 1998, and with Senate staffer, April 13, 1998.

11. Interview with congressional staffer on April 16, 1998, and House staffer, February 8, 1998. See also Office of the Secretary of Defense, "Information Paper," unpublished, on the frigates issue.

12. Interview with Department of Defense official, April 1, 1998. OSD "Information Paper" on the frigates issue.

13. Letter from Representative Benjamin Gilman and Representative Lee Hamilton to Secretary of State, April 3, 1996.

14. Letter from Senator Claiborne Pell to Secretary of State, April 18, 1996, and OSD "Information Paper" on the frigates issue.

15. Interview with congressional staffer, April 16, 1998.

16. Interviews with Senate staffer, April 16, 1998; Interview with Department of Defense official, September 14, 1998.

17. The extent of the president's involvement in trying to resolve the problem with Senator Paul Sarbanes differs significantly according to several different people whom I interviewed. Several agree that the president was asked to speak to Senator Sarbanes, and it appears he probably did, but that is difficult to confirm.

18. Interview with Senate staffer, April 13, 1998. Steve Forbes references this rumor in "Fact and Comment—How Bill Clinton Makes Foreign Policy," *Forbes,* April 21, 1997, p. 27.

19. Umit Enginsoy, "Turkey Shuts U.S. Firms Out of Defense Purchases / Officials Say No Sales until Frigates Are Freed," *Defense News,* vol. 12 (May 26, 1997), p. 11.

20. Interview with Department of Defense official, April 1, 1998.

21. Kelly Couturier, "Turkey Cancels Helicopter Purchase," *Washington Post,* November 28, 1996, p. A40.

22. Raymond Bonner, "U.S. Helicopter Sale to Turkey Hits Snag," *New York Times,* March 29, 1996, p. A10.

23. Enginsoy, "Turkey Shuts U.S. Firms Out of Defense Purchases," p. 11.

24. Letter from Senator Paul Sarbanes to President Clinton, February 19, 1997.

25. Letter from Senator Paul Sarbanes to President Clinton, February 19, 1997.

26. Interview with Senate staffer, April 13, 1998.

27. Enginsoy, "Turkey Shuts U.S. Firms Out of Defense Purchases."

28. Interview with Senate staffer, April 13, 1998. See also Umit Enginsoy and Philip Finnegan, "U.S. Assent on Greek Ships May Move Turkish Frigates," *Defense News,* vol. 12 (June 9, 1997), p. 4.

29. Interview with Senate staffer, April 16, 1998.

30. Interview with Department of Defense official, September 17, 1998, and with State Department of State official, October 26, 1998.

31. Interview with executive branch official, October 26, 1998.

32. Press statement by Deputy Spokesman James B. Foley on Meeting of Secretary of State Madeleine K. Albright with Greek Foreign Minister Pangalos and Turkish Foreign Minister Cem, Department of State, Office of the Spokesman, July 8, 1997.

33. Department of Defense, "Memorandum for Correspondents," press release 123-M, July 24, 1997.

Chapter Five

1. Section 620E of the Foreign Assistance Act of 1961 as amended by section 902 of the Nuclear Nonproliferation Conditions on Assistance for Pakistan of the International Security and Development Cooperation Act of 1985.

2. A useful summary of the history of the use of U.S. sanctions against Pakistan can be found in Dennis Kux, "Pakistan," in Richard N. Haass, ed., *Economic Sanctions and American Diplomacy* (New York: Council on Foreign Relations Press, 1998), pp. 157–176.

3. The Symington amendment (P. L. 90-629, Chapter 10—Nuclear Nonproliferation Controls, Sec. 101) prohibits U.S. assistance to any country that delivers or receives unsafeguarded "nuclear enrichment equipment, materials or technology." The president can waive these requirements by certifying to Congress that the "termination of such assistance would have a serious adverse effect on vital United States interests" and that "he has received reliable assurances that the country in question will not acquire or develop nuclear weapons or assist other countries in doing so." The Glenn amendment (P. L. 90-629, Chapter 10— Nuclear Nonproliferation Controls, Sec. 102 [1979 version]) prohibited U.S. assistance to any country that delivers or receives "nuclear reprocessing equipment, materials or technology" or receives, transfers, or detonates an explosive nuclear device. Again the president could waive the sanctions by certifying that the termination of assistance would be detrimental to U.S. nonproliferation objectives or "otherwise jeopardize the common defense and security." The Nuclear Proliferation Prevention Act of 1994 also sponsored by Senator Glenn sharply expanded this section to include broad, mandatory sanctions for any country that transfers a nuclear explosive device, receives a nuclear explosive device, or detonates such a device (P. L. 103-239, Chapter 10—Nuclear Nonproliferation Controls, Sec. 102B). A summary of the key legislative provisions affecting U.S. assistance to Pakistan can be found in Richard N. Haass and Gideon Rose, *A New U.S. Policy toward India and Pakistan*, Task Force Report (Council on Foreign Relations, Inc., 1997) and Richard Haass and Morton Halperin, *After the Tests: U.S. Policy toward India and Pakistan*, An Independent Task Force Report Co-sponsored by the Council on Foreign Relations and the Brookings Institution (September 1998).

4. Haass and Rose, *A New U.S. Policy toward India and Pakistan*, pp. 11–12. See also Shirin R. Tahir-Kheli, *India, Pakistan, and the United States: Breaking with the Past* (New York: Council on Foreign Relations Press, 1997), pp. 73–76.

5. Richard Whittle, "In Spite of Nuclear Issues: Congress Appears Willing to Approve Aid to Pakistan," *Congressional Quarterly Weekly Report*, vol. 39 (December 5, 1981), pp. 2411–14.

6. Statement by Senator Pressler in the *Congressional Record*, September 20, 1995, p. S13942. See also Tahir-Kheli, *India, Pakistan, and the United States*, p. 80.

7. Interview with U.S. government official, June 21, 1999.

8. Kux, "Pakistan," pp. 163–64.

9. Christopher Madison, "The Pakistan Conduit," *National Journal*, July 11, 1987, pp. 1773–75.

10. David Ottaway, "Addressing Congress, Bhutto Formally Renounces Nuclear Arms," *Washington Post,* June 8, 1989, p. A14.

11. Interview with U.S. government official, June 21, 1999.

12. Thomas W. Lippman, "Administration Proposes Compromise to Transfer Some Weapons to Pakistan," *Washington Post,* July 26, 1995, p. A19.

13. Interview with U.S. government official, June 21, 1999. And as described by Senator John Glenn, *Congressional Record,* September 20, 1995, p. S13961.

14. Carroll J. Doherty, "New Drive to Overhaul Aid Faces Perennial Obstacle," *Congressional Quarterly Weekly Report,* January 15, 1994, p. 74.

15. "Conditions for Resuming Economic Aid to Pakistan: A Historical Review of Executive Branch Assurances to Congress," *Congressional Record,* September 20, 1995, p. S13959.

16. Carroll J. Doherty, "Foreign Aid: Lawmakers Resist Effort to End Earmarks for Countries," *Congressional Quarterly Weekly Report,* February 5, 1994, p. 259.

17. Kux, "Pakistan," pp. 166–67.

18. Carroll J. Doherty, "Bid to Sell Jets to Pakistan May Provoke Fight on Hill," *Congressional Quarterly Weekly Report,* April 9, 1994, p. 851.

19. Interview with executive branch official, June 21, 1999.

20. Interview with Department of Defense official, April 6, 1998.

21. Sarah Walkling and Evan S. Medeiros, "Clinton, Bhutto Seek Resolution to 'Pressler' Ban on F-16 Deliveries," *Arms Control Today,* vol. 25 (May 1995), p. 24. A good explanation of the Pakistani position on the 1994 Talbott initiative can be found in Brian Cloughley, "Pakistan's Defence Strategy and the Nuclear Option Fanaticism," *Jane's Intelligence Review,* vol. 5, December 31, 1994, p. 115.

22. Cloughley, "Pakistan's Defense Strategy and the Nuclear Option Fanaticism."

23. Dana Priest, "U.S., Pakistan to Renew Talks: Perry Vows to Improve Military Relations despite Congressional Ban," *Washington Post,* January 11, 1995, p. A13.

24. "Establishing Strong Security Ties with India and Pakistan," speech by William J. Perry, before the Foreign Policy Association, New York, January 31, 1995.

25. Interview with Senate staffer, November 16, 1999.

26. Interview with Senate staffer, November 16, 1999.

27. R. Jeffrey Smith, "Defense and Diplomacy: Easing of Pakistan Policy Endorsed," *Washington Post,* March 10, 1995, p. A15.

28. *Overview of U.S. Policy toward South Asia,* Hearings before the Subcommittee on Near Eastern and South Asian Affairs of the Senate Committee on Foreign Relations, S. Hrg. 104-46, 104 Cong. 1 sess. (1995).

29. Interview with executive branch official, June 30, 1999.

30. Thomas W. Lippman and R. Jeffrey Smith, "Bhutto: Deliver F-16's or Return Payment: Pakistani Leader, in U.S., Has No Apologies for Nuclear Program," *Washington Post*, April 11, 1995, p. A15.

31. Press conference by the President and Prime Minister Benazir Bhutto of Pakistan, April 11, 1995, *Congressional Record*, June 30, 1995, p. S9568.

32. Interview with U.S. government official, June 21, 1999.

33. *Overview of U.S. Policy toward South Asia,* Hearings before the Subcommittee on Near Eastern and South Asian Affairs of the Senate Committee on Foreign Relations.

34. Interview with former congressional staffer, June 21, 1999.

35. Interview with former congressional staffer, June 21, 1999.

36. Thomas W. Lippman, "Compromise Proposed on Fighter Sale to Pakistan," *Washington Post*, May 24, 1995, p. A8; and *The Foreign Aid Reduction Act of 1995*, S. Rpt. 104-99, 104 Cong. 1 sess. (1995).

37. Thomas W. Lippman, "Administration Proposes Compromise to Transfer Some Weapons to Pakistan," *Washington Post,* July 26, 1995, p. A19.

38. *Conventional Weapons and Foreign Policy in South Asia,* Hearing before the Subcommittee on Near Eastern and South Asian Affairs of the Senate Committee on Foreign Relations, S. Hrg. 104-226, 104 Cong. 1 sess. (1995).

39. Hank Brown in *Congressional Record*, September 20, 1995, p. S13925. See also Thomas W. Lippman, "Bhutto Receives Clinton Promise of Aid; President Says He Will Ask Hill to Help Release F-16 Fighters for Delivery to Pakistan," *Washington Post*, April 12, 1995, p. A1.

40. Brown in *Congressional Record*, September 20, 1995, p. S13926.

41. Carroll J. Doherty, "Senate Votes to End 5-Year Ban on Direct Aid to Pakistan," *Congressional Quarterly Weekly Report*, September 23, 1995, pp. 2921–24.

42. Interview with former congressional staffer, June 21, 1999.

43. Thomas W. Lippman and Dan Morgan, "With Clinton Approval, Senate Votes to End Ban on Arms Shipment to Pakistan," *Washington Post*, September 22, 1995, p. A5.

44. Thomas W. Lippman, "Conferees Loosen Ban on Arms to Pakistan, Soften Senate Language on Russia," *Washington Post*, October 25, 1995, p. A6.

45. Frank Pallone in *Congressional Record*, October 31, 1995, p. H11565.

46. See statements by Chairman Livingston and others in the *Congressional Record*, October 31, 1995, pp. 11527, 11565.

47. Interview with former congressional staffer, June 21, 1999.

48. R. Jeffrey Smith, "Proliferation Concerns May Delay U.S. Arms Shipment to Pakistan," *Washington Post*, February 15, 1996, p. A23.

49. R. Jeffrey Smith, "U.S. May Waive Sanctions on China for Sale Related to Nuclear Arms," *Washington Post*, February 8, 1996, p. A20; Paul Blustein and R. Jeffrey Smith, "Economic, Political Concerns Put Clinton on the Spot in China Policy," *Washington Post*, February 11, 1996, p. A26. R. Jeffrey Smith, "U.S. Decides to Transfer Weapons That Pakistan Paid for in 1980's," *Washington Post*, March 20, 1996, p. A27.

50. Interview with executive branch official, June 21, 1999.

51. Thomas W. Lippman, "U.S. Clears Pakistan, China Deals," *Washington Post*, April 17, 1996, p. A28.

52. Interview with administration official, April 6, 1998.

53. Ibid.

54. Thomas W. Lippman, "U.S. to Sell Jets to Indonesia, Transfer Proceeds to Pakistan," *Washington Post*, June 5, 1996, p. A27.

55. Keith B. Richburg, "Indonesia Drops Plans to Buy U.S. F16s; Jakarta Cites Congressional Criticism of Its Human Rights Record," *Washington Post*, June 7, 1997, p. A1. Also, Steven Erlanger, "U.S. May Halt Sale of Jets to Indonesia," *New York Times*, August 21, 1996, p. A7.

56. Interview with administration official, June 14, 1999.

57. Interview with Senate staffer, November 16, 1999.

58. Interview with former congressional staffer, June 21, 1999.

59. Interview with former congressional staffer, June 21, 1999.

60. Dan Morgan and Kevin Marida, "South Asia Rivals Had Money on South Dakota Senate Race; Ethnic Donors Play Powerful Role in U.S. Politics," *Washington Post*, March 24, 1997, p. A1.

61. Interview with former congressional staffer, June 21, 1999.

Chapter Six

1. Article I, Convention on the Prohibition of the Development, Production, Stockpiling, and Use of Chemical Weapons and on Their Destruction (Chemical Weapons Convention).

2. Amy E. Smithson, "Dateline Washington: Clinton Fumbles the CWC," *Foreign Policy*, no. 99 (Summer 1995), p. 171.

3. This analysis draws heavily from news accounts, *Congressional Quarterly Weekly Reports*, and interviews with congressional staff and administration officials who were involved with the ratification effort. A useful summary of the issues involved can be found in Mary H. Cooper, "Chemical and Biological Weapons: Should the U.S. Sign the New Treaty?" *Congressional Quarterly Researcher*, vol. 7 (January 31, 1997), pp. 73–96. A fairly comprehensive story of the ratification process (admittedly from the perspective of some of the treaty's staunchest supporters) can be found in Michael Krepon, Amy E. Smithson, and John Parachini, "The Battle to Obtain U.S. Ratification of the Chemi-

cal Weapons Convention," Occasional Paper 35 (Washington: Henry L. Stimson Center, July 1997).

4. Interviews with administration officials on April 1, 1998, and September 14, 1998.

5. Interview with administration official, September 14, 1998. See also David C. Morrison, "Political Chemistry," *National Journal*, vol. 26 (May 14, 1994), pp. 1131–33 for a brief explanation of the chemical demilitarization issue.

6. Interview with former administration official, September 29, 1998.

7. Smithson, "Dateline Washington: Clinton Fumbles the CWC," pp. 168–82.

8. Interview with administration official, April 1, 1998.

9. Morrison, "Political Chemistry," p. 1131.

10. Interview with administration official, April 1, 1998.

11. Interview with Senate staffer, April 13, 1998.

12. A fairly detailed analysis of the various State Department reorganization efforts during this time frame can be found in James M. Lindsay, "The State Department Complex after the Cold War," in Randall B. Ripley and James M. Lindsay, eds., *U.S. Foreign Policy after the Cold War* (University of Pittsburgh Press, 1997), pp. 74–105.

13. Interview with Senate staffer, April 13, 1998.

14. Lindsay, "The State Department Complex after the Cold War," p. 97.

15. Helen Dewar, "Flag Amendment Blocked in Senate: Democrat Tries to Force Helms to Act on Treaty, 18 Nominations," *Washington Post*, December 7, 1995, p. A15.

16. Thomas W. Lippman, "Helms Ends Impasse on Most Envoy Nominations: Both Parties Claim Victory as Vote Set on Foreign Policy Reorganization That Had Blocked Action," *Washington Post*, September 30, 1995, p. A9.

17. Dewar, "Flag Amendment Blocked in Senate," p. A15; Helen Dewar, "Senate Deal on Foreign Policy Agencies Ends Impasse on Envoys, Treaties," *Washington Post*, December 8, 1995, p. A20; and Helen Dewar, "Senate Sends Ambassadors to Work: Arms, Chemical Pacts Also Move Ahead," *Washington Post*, December 15, 1995, p. A34.

18. Interview with Senate staffer, April 13, 1998.

19. Pat Towell, "Arms Control: Administration Begins New Drive for Chemical Weapons Treaty," *Congressional Quarterly Weekly Report*, March 30, 1996, pp. 893–94.

20. Elizabeth Palmer, "Arms Control: Senate Panel Opens Hearings on Chemical Weapons Pact," *Congressional Quarterly Weekly Report*, March 26, 1994, p. 756; and Towell, "Administration Begins New Drive for Chemical Weapons Treaty," pp. 893–94.

21. Interview with Senate staffer, April 21, 1998. See also R. Jeffrey Smith, "Defense and Diplomacy—Chemical Arms Pact Backed," *Washington Post*, April 26, 1996, p. A18.

22. Interview with Senate staffer, April 13, 1998.

23. Pat Towell, "Defense Authorization: Senate Puts Off Missile Debate, Clearing Way for Defense Bill," *Congressional Quarterly Weekly Report*, June 29, 1996, pp. 1884–85.

24. Interview with administration official, September 14, 1998.

25. Interview with administration official, April 1, 1998.

26. William J. Perry and Janet Reno, "A Treaty in the U.S. Interest," *Washington Post*, September 11, 1996, p. A23.

27. Interview with Senate staffer, April 13, 1998.

28. Amy E. Smithson, "Bungling a No-Brainer," in Krepon, Smithson, and Parachini, "The Battle to Obtain U.S. Ratification of the Chemical Weapons Convention," Occasional Paper 35, p. 21.

29. Thomas W. Lippman, "Senate Foes Derail Chemical Weapons Treaty," *Washington Post*, September 13, 1996, p. A1; and Pat Towell, "Arms Control: Chemical Weapons Ban Delayed as Dole Joins Objectors," *Congressional Quarterly Weekly Report*, September 14, 1996, pp. 2607–08.

30. Interview with administration official, September 14, 1998.

31. Amy E. Smithson and Laurie H. Boulden, "Chemical Weapons: Neglected Menace," *Issues in Science and Technology*, vol. 12 (Spring 1996), p. 81.

32. Interview with Senate staffer, April 21, 1998. See also Smithson, "Bungling a No-Brainer," p. 16.

33. Interview with Senate staffer, April 13, 1998.

34. Interview with administration official, September 14, 1998.

35. Interview with Senate staffer, April 13, 1998. For public hardball see Thomas W. Lippman, "Helms to Delay Vote on Chemical Arms Pact: Panel Chairman Puts GOP 'Priorities' First," *Washington Post*, February 4, 1997, p. A1; Thomas W. Lippman, "Unmodified, Chemical Weapons Pact Is Doomed, Sen. Helms Warns," *Washington Post*, March 9, 1997, p. A10; and Thomas W. Lippman, "White House Has Rally for Weapons Ban: Sen. Helms Offers List of Treaty Opponents," *Washington Post*, April 5, 1997, p. A8.

36. Interview with Senate staffers, April 13 and April 21, 1998.

37. Interview with Senate staffer, April 16, 1998.

38. Interview with U.S. government official, June 30, 1999.

39. Interview with administration official, April 1, 1998.

40. Interview with U.S. government official, June 30, 1999.

41. John Parachini, "NGOs: Force Multipliers in the CWC Ratification Debate," in Krepon, Smithson, and Parachini, "The Battle to Obtain U.S. Ratification of the Chemical Weapons Convention," Occasional Paper 35, p. 39.

42. Lippman, "White House Has Rally for Weapons Ban: Sen. Helms Offers List of Treaty Opponents," p. A8.

43. Interview with Senate staffer, April 21, 1998.

44. Pat Towell and Chuck McCutcheon, "Senate Moves toward Vote on Chemical Arms Pact," *Congressional Quarterly Weekly Report*, April 12, 1997, pp. 853–55; and Smithson, "Bungling a No-Brainer," p. 27.

45. Helen Dewar, "Senate Sets Chemical Arms Pact Vote: After 4 Years of Delay, Action on Treaty Is Scheduled for Next Week," *Washington Post*, April 18, 1997, p. A10; and John F. Harris and Thomas W. Lippman, "Clinton Agrees to Shift Foreign Policy Agencies: Move Comes as Senate Sets Chemical Arms Vote," *Washington Post*, April 18, 1997, p. A1.

46. Interview with Senate staffer, April 21, 1998.

47. Interview with Senate staffer, April 16, 1998, and with administration official on September 14, 1998. For news account see Helen Dewar, "Dole Raises Hopes of Chemical Treaty Backers: Former Clinton Rival Announces Support on Eve of Vote: Lott Offers Conciliatory Words on Pact," *Washington Post*, April 24, 1997, p. A1.

48. Interview with Senate staffer, April 13, 1998.

49. Interview with Senate staffer, April 21, 1998.

50. John F. Harris and Helen Dewar, "Chemical Weapons Treaty in Peril, Democrats Fear: Clinton Says U.S. Risks Joining 'Pariah Nations,'" *Washington Post*, April 19, 1997, p. A1.

51. Pat Towell, "Chemical Weapons Ban Approved in Burst of Compromise," *Congressional Quarterly Weekly Report*, April 26, 1997, pp. 973–74, 976; Peter Baker, "Clinton-Lott Connection Emerges in Treaty Fight: After Chemical Pact, Other Tough Tests Await," *Washington Post*, April 26, 1997, p. A1; Donna Cassata, "For Lott, a Chance to Rise Above the Fray," *Congressional Quarterly Weekly Report*, April 26, 1997, p. 975; and Helen Dewar, "Senate Approves Chemical Arms Pact after Clinton Pledge," *Washington Post*, April 25, 1997, p. A1.

52. Pat Towell, "Senate Passes Bill to Enforce Chemical Weapons Ban," *Congressional Quarterly Weekly Report*, May 24, 1997, p. 1207.

53. Smithson, "Bungling a No-Brainer," pp. 7–33.

54. Morrison, "Political Chemistry," p. 1131.

55. Interview with Senate staffer, April 19. 1998.

56. Interview with former administration official, July 23, 1998.

57. Chuck McCutcheon, "Senate Prepares to Take Up Nuclear Test Ban Treaty; Ratification Still a Long Shot," *Congressional Quarterly Weekly Report*, October 2, 1999, pp. 2325–2326.

58. Chuck McCutcheon, "Treaty Vote a 'Wake-Up Call'," *Congressional Quarterly Weekly Report*, October 16, 1999, pp. 2435–2438.

59. Helen Dewar, "Senate Rejects Test Ban Treaty," *Washington Post*, October 14, 1999, p. A1.

Chapter Seven

1. Chuck McCutcheon, "Treaty Vote A 'Wake-Up Call,'" *Congressional Quarterly Weekly Report*, October 16, 1999, p. 2435.

2. Lee H. Hamilton, "The Role of Congress in U.S. Foreign Policy," speech before the Center for Strategic and International Studies, November 19, 1998, Washington.

3. Carroll J. Doherty, "Senate Caught in the Grip of its Own 'Holds' System," *Congressional Quarterly Weekly Report*, August 15, 1998, p. 2241.

4. Al Kamen, "Party Tensions," *Washington Post*, July 22, 1998, p. A15.

Index